D1108559

Toulouse-Lautrec *His Complete Lithographs and Drypoints*

Jean Adhémar

Toulouse-Lautrec

His Complete Lithographs and Drypoints

Harry N. Abrams, Inc., Publishers, New York

Jacket design by Wim Crouwel
Library of Congress Catalog Card Number: 65–21831

Harry N. Abrams, Inc. New York
Printed and bound in Japan

CONTENTS

PREFACE

Toulouse-Lautrec would hardly have been surprised by a special tribute to his graphic work, and it would certainly have pleased him. Indeed, he received such tributes in his own lifetime; from the moment he began exhibiting lithographs and designing posters, both public and officials paid him homage. And he was always particularly sensitive to praise for his graphic work, on which he had set his heart.

Maindron and Arsène Alexandre were among those who praised the line, the flair and the daring layout of his lithographs. These have been studied and reproduced by Marcel Guérin, Claude Roger-Marx, Robert Rey and, more recently, by Mme Dortu and Philippe Huisman. But for a long time the definitive work on them was Loÿs Delteil's two-volume study, published in 1920 in his series, *Le peintre-graveur illustré* (vols. X and XI). Delteil reproduced 368 lithographs, zinc engravings and posters; in addition to dates, he provided footnotes and information on printings, collections and sale prices. This valuable work is now out of print and virtually unobtainable; in any case, for obvious reasons, it is somewhat dated. Not only have many of the works changed hands since the book appeared, but there has been a great deal of subsequent work done on Lautrec, particularly between the wars. All the same, it remains the cornerstone of studies on Lautrec's graphic work, and I am grateful for its help.

The present catalogue does not follow the traditional chronology, and in dating the later works it diverges considerably from Delteil—not just in order to be different, but because Delteil's work is now partially obsolete in spite of its tremendous merit. Prints have reappeared bearing unarguable dates, and it has become generally easier to say when a given play was staged or a particular book written or published. I have also attempted to classify Lautrec's works by the date they were executed rather than the date they were published, if there was a significant interval between the two. Finally, no one has yet taken sufficient account of a phenomenon which Lautrec's friends found most striking: the sudden passion he would develop for a person, a woman, an animal, a gesture, or some form of pleasure. Moreover, his friends emphasized the essentially fleeting nature of these infatuations; his models must often have been bewildered and distressed when, after continually seeking them out, admiring and drawing them, Lautrec would suddenly drop them, announcing that he 'needed a change'. Except for Jane Avril and Joyant, Lautrec was never attached to his friends, or actresses, or women, for more than a few months, and sometimes for only a few days. Because of this, dates of publication need to be treated with caution. Works in which one model figures should be grouped together, even when they were published at intervals of months. Marcelle Lender, for example, represents a period of a few weeks in Lautrec's life during which time he went to see her act in *Chilpéric* every night. And Marthe Brandès took up a few days in 1894. Then there was the phase of Calmèse (he rented out horses in the rue Fontaine), and the phases of Palmyre's fat bull-dog Bouboule, of Robin's collie, and of the little bull-terrier. The publication dates are of secondary importance for another reason: there is nothing to prove that Lautrec, especially towards the end of his life, executed a lithograph just before its publication.

I have reclassified Lautrec's work, with these thoughts in mind, along more coherent and firmer lines. It does not necessarily end in 1901, but perhaps earlier, with a series on race-horses in 1899. This takes into account his state of health; he could hardly work at all in his last years, as his contemporaries have noted.

Like Delteil, I have listed only Lautrec's original works, discarding the facsimiles of drawings and the plates from *Le Rire*, of which there exist separate printings done afterwards without lettering on white paper. These were passed off as original lithographs, though they fetched a very low price between 1900 and 1910. But this book, which claims to list all of Lautrec's original works, is more complete than Delteil because a few additional examples have been rediscovered.

From time to time, I have deliberately used a version of a print before lettering, as well as one after lettering, in order to illustrate the differences that cannot be seen in Delteil's book, which usually shows only the final print.

I must thank those who have helped me: first, Gerstenberg's heir, Walter Scharf. Gerstenberg had bought some very rare lithographs from Mutiaux and from Sagot; of some of these, which often came from Stern, only one known copy exists. M. Jean-Claude Romand must also be thanked; as his grandmother, Mme Le Garrec, did ten years ago, he let me have the notes Sagot made on the Lautrec works that passed through his hands between 1890 and 1910. M. Paul Prouté provided helpful suggestions and was kind enough to spend an evening of work with me.

I have used the studies of Gerstle Mack, Roger-Marx and Perruchot. They, in their turn, used my catalogue of the Lautrec exhibition that took place at the Bibliothèque Nationale in 1955. That catalogue was a systematic attempt at a historical dating.

Many of the texts I have cited are the work of journalists, and are often unknown to historians. They come mostly from the humorous paper, *Fin de Siècle*, the faithful chronicler of Lautrec and doubtless his own reading-matter.

My colleagues in France and abroad have also helped me a great deal. Mlle Damiron, Curator of the Bibliothèque d'Art et d'Archéologie; Mr Bjurström, Curator of the Stockholm National Museum; Dr Franke Steenbock, at the print-room of the Staatliche Museum, Berlin-Dahlem; Dr Van Heisinger, of the Kunsthalle, Bremen; Dr Ade, Director of the Haus der Kunst, Munich; Frau Billeter, Curator of the Kunstgewerbe Museum, Zürich; and especially Herr Werner Schmidt, Curator of Prints, Dresden.

I decided not to re-read the work that I wrote with Francis Jourdain, published in 1952; I was determined to use new sources, so as to avoid repetition. This will, anyway, be my last book on Lautrec. The new generation of critics will have to study more closely the remarkable observations by B. Nicholson in *Burlington Magazine* (1951, p. 229) and produce a morphological study of Lautrec's art. It is all too easy to put Lautrec in a category by himself, when our first task should be to relate him to his contemporaries: Carrière, Gauguin, Cézanne and Munch.

Lautrec was determined to use engraving as a medium of expression. Not being a professional, he naturally did not think of engraving with an etcher's needle. He might have liked etching, but the great publisher of etchings, Cadart, had died in 1875, and his widow went bankrupt in 1882. In addition, the Société des Aquafortistes had fallen into a state of decline, and the public had come to reject a medium that was no longer used by artists, but only by amateurs. There remained only lithography. Degas, always Lautrec's idol, was a master of this medium. The young artists Maurice Denis, Vuillard and Bonnard also worked in lithography, and they were to show Lautrec the way.

Lithography in black and white, and especially in colour, had one enthusiastic advocate, who wanted to make the public appreciate it. This was Mellerio, the young art critic and friend of Durand-Ruel. The articles of Roger-Marx, the activity of publishers like Vollard and of dealers like Kleinmann and Sagot, also helped to bring lithography into favour.

It is not easy for us to understand the status of engraving which, about 1880, was fancied by numerous collectors and the trade alike. Engravings circulated in France and abroad; due to them rather than to paintings, the school of young artists enjoyed a public that could not afford to buy paintings. At that time, the engravers were already stressing the value of an original print, done by the hand of the artist himself without using any mechanical process. But the public resisted at first and could not clearly grasp the difference between an original and its reproduction in a magazine. So the artists started working for the newspapers, and the press tried to convince people that it was producing works of commercial value—a claim that did not take in the genuine collectors.

What sort of man was this Lautrec who, around 1890, began doing graphic work, using lithography as his medium? Perhaps he was the 'fallen women's Goya', as recent articles have tried to maintain. Above all, though, he was an *expressionist*, one of the very first French expressionists after Daumier. His famous slogan, 'Ah, life!' is the keynote: he was trying to express life in all its guises. He looked for the least traditional, the least banal of its forms, for these were more striking. Too little attention has been paid to his frequent explanations that he did not go into the world of prostitutes and Montmartre café-concerts as an explorer, a traveller, or even as a pleasure-seeker, but as a historian. The expression of life which he found there, he found also in the theatre, and it is hardly accidental that half the subjects of Lautrec's graphic work are actors. This has not been adequately stressed, in spite of an excellent article by Jean Nepveu-Degas on the subject. To his friends' surprise, Lautrec would go to the theatre not to listen to the plays, but to capture the actors' features, sharpened by make-up, from angles that showed them up best under stage lighting.

His ardent pursuit of expressionism began towards 1890—in other words, in the heyday of impressionism. Lautrec had been under the spell of that movement, but he had given it up. This did not escape the notice of his friends and contemporaries. In *Peints à leur tour* (p. 159), Thadée Natanson stressed the singularity of Lautrec's subjects, the way he brought out their deportment and threw them into relief, his 'stalking of the unusual'. The public appreciated the beauty and the colour-effects in his posters more than his portrayal of the human face. His models, from Yvette Guilbert to Marcelle Lender, often said that they regretted his harshness; nor did they understand that they owed to him their chance of survival, for, except in the case of Bruant and Jane Avril, his vision of them surpassed their actual stage performance. Yvette Guilbert, who deformed her face, Bruant, and Nicolle, who was called 'a Daumier', ended by accepting him because he conveyed what they were trying to express on stage.

Standing aloof from the impressionists, Lautrec, in his graphic art, also remained on the fringe of the Nabi movement, in spite of his friendship with Vuillard and his admiration for Bonnard as a poster artist. The Natansons probably cared for him more as a wit and entertainer than as an artist. True, they did commission him to do a poster for the *Revue Blanche;* but they did not say whether they were satisfied with it, while the public attacked the poster for making no attempt to canvass subscriptions. At heart, Natanson was surprised that he saw Lautrec so rarely at the magazine's offices or at the rue Laffitte.

All this explains Lautrec's isolation, and his relegation to the world of minor Montmartre artists, such as Somm, the cartoonist, and the bohemian engraver, Charles Maurin. Both these men, incidentally. stood much higher than Lautrec in the esteem of newspaper directors and journalists.

As he was relatively cut off and yet needed the human contact so important in his art, Lautrec tried to get through to the public. He exhibited at the Indépendants and sent his work to the Vingt de Bruxelles; but he seems to have been especially careful about what he sent to engravers' associations, like the Peintres-Graveurs Français, to exhibitions like the Lithography Centenary, and to displays like the Rheims poster exhibition.

A study of Lautrec's literary contacts reveals, in the *Revue Blanche* circle, a close acquaintance with Tristan Bernard. Bernard was also linked to the humorist Alphonse Allais, who was rediscovered before Bernard and had much the same cast of mind.

In 1892, Allais gave his *nouvelles* the title *Vive la vie*, which recalls Lautrec's motto. Like Tristan Bernard, Allais was close to Romain Coolus, the friend whom Lautrec called Colette. Allais was also on good terms with Maurice Donnay, whose Montmartre songs were illustrated by Lautrec. But the great man of this circle was Jules Renard, and Lautrec admired him tremendously. This admiration was not returned, probably from a kind of instinctive jealousy on Renard's part.

All these humorists would meet at the theatre, where Lucien Guitry, Jeanne Granier, Marthe Brandès and Lugné-Poë were their idols, as they were Lautrec's.

It is worth remembering that any tour of the world of expressionist writers and theatre always returns to Lautrec.

1885

Lautrec's first graphic work was a zinc engraving dated 1885 by Delteil. It was the cover of one of Aristide Bruant's most famous ballads, *A Saint-Lazare*. Lautrec was still working at Cormon's, painting a great deal, 'very busy', as his mother put it; and he was installed in Montmartre where Bruant, in his cabaret Le Mirliton, exerted a fascination over him.

Bruant had this engraving printed in his magazine, *Le Mirliton*, in August 1887. He later had a painting and several drawings by Lautrec reproduced in the same magazine: *Le Dernier Salut* (Salut au corbillard), *La Dernière Goutte* and *Sur le Pavé*.

1891

In the years that followed, Lautrec worked for the *Courrier Français*, whose director, Jules Roques, was a lively businessman and discoverer of new talent. He asked Lautrec for some drawings and published several, among them *Gin Cocktail*. The rest he sold at auction, and this understandably outraged Lautrec. Other drawings were used in the 7 July 1888 issue of *Paris Illustré*, to illustrate an article by J. Michelet on 'Summer in Paris'. Still others were refused by *La Chronique Médicale* in 1891. Gauzi recalled that, at the time, 'while he was still almost unknown, Lautrec tried to place his drawings with newspaper publishers', less to earn a living than to make a name for himself. For his public was still limited, and he could acquire a quick reputation through the newspapers, which were then so widely read—a point Philippe Huisman has rightly stressed.

Lautrec did no graphic work between 1889 and 1891. In those years he was painting a great deal, and his career as an engraver really dates only from 1891. Duret saw clearly that this beginning coincided with the maturity of the twenty-eight-year-old painter's talent, which Mirbeau acknowledged in the *Echo de Paris* on 31 May 1891. He wrote that Lautrec brought 'a genuine spiritual and tragic force to the study of faces and the penetration of character', adding that his work was 'striking for its assurance, its flexibility, and its ease of execution.' Mirbeau also pointed out that Lautrec was fascinated by colour lithography and eager to succeed in that field.

Lautrec's first colour lithograph was his poster for the Moulin Rouge, commissioned by its director, Zidler. The Moulin Rouge had recently opened and was highly successful. It was 'definitely the gayest music-hall in Paris. Lucky Zidler!' wrote the *Fin de Siècle* on 5 September 1891. Lucien Muhfeld was to use the picturesque Zidler, under the name of Zessler, as one of the characters in his novel, *La Carrière d'André Tourette* (1900). Here Zidler is described as the 'protector of the frivolous arts and of the nation's pleasure', a man who understood that his profession must be based on 'the naïveté, the lewdness, and the laziness of men.' Women were for him 'perverse, irresponsible little bitches'.

Lautrec had thought of doing posters because he found it difficult to exhibit his paintings, and even more difficult to show his prints. Besides, in those days a poster was regarded as a work of art. It was a commonplace for a journalist to claim, as one did in *Le Figaro* as early as 1885, that 'there can be more talent in a poster than in many a painting which creates a sensation.' The greatest poster artist of the day, Chéret, 'admired by policemen and people of taste alike', had been decorated—a fantastic honour at that time. At the peak of his career and his art—he was forty-five then, and was to live on, blind, to the age of ninety-five—Chéret himself (interviewed in 1892) named Lautrec as his successor and heir. 'Lautrec is a master,' he said; and out of gratitude, Lautrec had himself photographed removing his hat in front of one of Chéret's posters. In fact, Lautrec's work did not stem from Chéret but far more from the Nabi painters, especially Bonnard, whose poster *France-Champagne* (according to Roger-Marx) preceded Lautrec's *Moulin Rouge*, and was thus the first modern poster after Daumier's *Le Charbonnier* (*c.* 1873). Unfortunately Roger-Marx is the only authority for pre-dating Bonnard's poster; no confirmation has yet been found in any text or document. (The *Moulin Rouge* was not registered at the Cabinet des Estampes, where the records would have provided a date.)

This poster, deliberately brutal and simplified, in which everything is stripped to essentials, caused an immediate sensation. Until then, people had been accustomed to a clever layout from which a coy face, with yellow, pink and green tints left over, so to speak, from the 18th century, would look out with false modesty. Here, recalling the Japanese and also his friends the Nabi painters, Lautrec made La Goulue's drawers dazzling—the poster said they could be seen 'every night' at the Moulin Rouge. This scandalous white underwear was, in fact, definitely toned down from the show itself, as so often described in the popular press.

La Goulue's strange dancing partner, Valentin, appears in the foreground of the poster. This black sheep of a solicitor's family was a dance-mad amateur, who worked in a bar next to the Place des Victoires during the day. This method of making the faces of his models more expressive by drawing them in silhouette was one of Lautrec's trademarks for a time, but he soon gave it up.

In the background, silhouetted against the gas-lights like Chinese shadow puppets, Lautrec's friends, his doctor cousin and the strange Jane Avril, can be seen among the Moulin Rouge regulars.

Camille Lemonnier's article in *Fin de Siècle* on 26 August shows how precisely Lautrec caught the scene. When the orchestra 'struck up the Saxony salvo' after the concert, Lemonnier saw La Goulue (he calls her Fruchette) doing the splits to make 'the joker's St Andrew Cross'. She was surrounded under the 'glaring electric light' by 'the compact mass of a hedge of faces—old, rather overripe men's faces and girls' pert faces plastered a foot thick in white.' Muhfeld also emphasized the effect of the electric bulbs, which shed 'a dazzling, fake daylight of wan whites and brutal shadows, an artificial and pseudo-theatrical glare.'

La Goulue had a triumphant but brief career. By the end of 1891, the popular press was already raving about those who were imitating her and Valentin in Paris and in the provinces, such as La Margotte and Magloire in Caen. The painter Gauzi saw her at the Moulin Rouge at the same time as Lautrec, his friend: 'With her helmet of blond hair and a décolletage down to her navel, she would enter the dance-hall like a conqueror. She danced with a guttersnipe's elegance, and knew how to show off her legs by performing clever cross-kicks; her skirts, hitched up to her waist, revealed the perfection of those legs. Decency was preserved by a pair of transparent muslin drawers that prevented no one from seeing her fair body.'

Valentin, whose real name was Edme-Etienne Renaudin, was forty-seven years old, according to an interview in *L'Eclair* on 29 December 1902; Duret said that 'he defied imitation. He was a thin, elongated man whose agility and vigour were concentrated in his legs. He would flap them incessantly, forcing them into a kind of choppy undulation. He was the opposite of Lautrec, with his stunted legs, and Lautrec must have envied him. As for La Goulue, she danced with the skilled fury of unbridled improvization.'

1892

Before April in the year 1892, the Boussod and Valadon gallery commissioned two big colour lithographs of the Moulin Rouge from Lautrec. They were put up for sale that October. One of them is wrongly known as *La Goulue et sa sœur*, and the other is likewise mistitled *L'Anglais au Moulin Rouge*. The first actually shows La Goulue with her friend 'la môme Fromage', a little seamstress who later became a star. The second is of an English impresario, named W. T. Warner, who went over to France to sign up café-concert performers; this is why Lautrec showed him being flattered by the two women in the picture and called it *Flirt*. Perhaps Lautrec thought of the two lithographs as complementary: the *Flirt* of Warner set against the insolent pose of La Goulue and her friend. These two prints, huge for their period, are among the best and rarest of Lautrec's colour lithographs. *La Goulue et sa sœur* captures the exact feeling of a painting.

Next to appear were *Le Pendu* (April), a poster in grey and white on the Calas affair, and *Reine de Joie* (May or early June), a bookshop poster advertising a novel by Victor Joze, which had a Bonnard cover. Not unrelated to the La Goulue poster, this shows a young woman, Hélène Roland, the heroine of the book, kissing the fat Olizac as he leaves Paris. This poster caused a scandal in banking circles, and a party of young stockbrokers tore it off the walls. Others bribed the billstickers to hand over the posters to them. The matter went so far that the Chief of Police called on the head of the Bonnard-Bidault publicity firm to make enquiries, and ordered the arrest of two tactless bill-stickers. The reason for all this was the intervention of Baron de Rothschild, who thought he recognized himself in the hero of the book, Baron de Rosenfeld, and wanted to stop the sale of this anti-Semitic work. The newspaper which reported the story bought up the remaining prints of the poster and put them up for sale, probably for anti-Semitic purposes.

Lautrec executed two more posters in 1892, both of Bruant in his cabaret. Bruant had stopped performing on the boulevard Rochechouart; but its atmosphere was recreated at Les Ambassadeurs, where he opened on 3 June 1892. In Montmartre, the man with the black hat and red scarf had delighted the snobs by giving them the rough edge of his tongue. His number in the café-concerts of the Champs-Elysées was just as successful. He had known Lautrec for a long time, and asked him for the poster which Ducarre, the manager of Les Ambassadeurs, reluctantly accepted on condition that he did not have to pay for the original drawing or the printing.

Gauzi, who was present when Lautrec drew it, was surprised to see Bruant pose and 'talk simply, without slang'. According to Gauzi, it was not Bruant who launched Lautrec, but the other way round: Lautrec's poster, with its brutal blocks of red and black against a white background, 'made Bruant's profile known to all Paris.'

Maurice Joyant mentions other projected posters of Bruant which were never carried out, particularly one with a back view of the singer facing an audience.

1893

In January 1893, when Lautrec's best friend, Doctor Bourges, was married, the two men had to part. This disturbed Lautrec deeply. He was afraid of being alone; he needed a close friend, a confidant, who was also a protector. His cousin, Doctor Gabriel Tapié de Céleyran, then Maurice Guibert, then Dethomas, were to play this role. Lautrec needed a companion like the one described in *Papa*, the 1911 comedy by de Flers and Caillavet: 'I follow you through your life. For twenty years I've been following you. You are no longer at an age when I can change my habits... You've always given me half your joys. In exchange, I've given you half my troubles. That makes us even.'

Meanwhile, Lautrec's mother had moved into the rue de Douai and he took his meals there. He does not appear to have been doing much work, though he did have his first exhibition, together with the artist Maurin, at Joyant's, 19 boulevard Montmartre, in February. Degas declared himself satisfied with the show, and *L'Eclair* reviewed it in an article on 2 February, saying that Charles Maurin had been the better-known of the two painters 'for a number of years' (an undeserved distinction). As for Lautrec, 'we know his studies of our customs, which he does in such personal, spicy colours; his dry humour has a slyness which we would now call cocking a snook; he can put all this into his posters, with his very new pictorial flair.' In *La Justice*, Gustave Geffroy said that 'his posters have triumphed in the streets with their irresistible mastery'; he admired Lautrec's bold and frank 'philosophy of vice'. In *Le Rapide*, Roger-Marx, who was from that time on one of Lautrec's most fervent admirers, compared his interest in gesture and psychology to that of Huysmans and Henri Becque.

In February or early March 1893, André Marty published Lautrec's picture of Loie Fuller. It was an extremely finished piece of work on which Lautrec had worked hard. He had pulled at least four versions in black, and had finally printed fifty copies, which he himself had hand-tinted and dusted over with gold powder. He had also coloured the mask around the print.

Lautrec showed the dancer exactly as his contemporaries saw her: 'a mist of veils' lit up by electricity (Michel Zévaco); 'a whirlwind of draperies' (Goncourt), 'floating like a ghost' on the stage of the Folies-Bergère. She was lit by the very first electric floodlights, installed specially for her. Jean Lorrain described her in *L'Echo de Paris littéraire et illustré*, on 4 December 1893, as 'that beautiful girl, in swirls of skirts, who spins and spins, swooning in the burning lights.' Loie Fuller had come to Paris in October 1892, after an enthusiastic reception in her native United States. Unable to appear at the Opéra, she had to be satisfied with the Folies-Bergère. There she danced her 'serpentine' or fire dance which became famous. According to *La Vie Parisienne* on 14 March 1893, she even started a fashion, the Loie Fuller skirt. Things went still further: in *Toute ma vie* (I), Mistinguett says, 'Loie Fuller invented the métro style. She whirled in spirals like a fountain; they called her "the electric fairy". Edison used to say, "My sister, Loie". Her dancing started the modern style.'

No one knows what Loie Fuller thought of Lautrec. She does not seem to have appreciated her young admirer; she asked Chéret to do her poster, of course, and wanted Reutlinger to photograph her, as those were the two celebrities of the moment. De Feure, Lucas and Pal, the fashionable illustrators and poster artists, were also to work for her.

At about this time, in February, Lautrec did a poster for an English paper firm, Bella Brothers, who organized poster exhibitions in London in 1895 and 1896, and asked for something from him. In this poster, *Confetti*, Lautrec alters his style; it is more akin to Bonnard's. Confetti had been the delight of the people of Paris during Mardi Gras, but was then banned. The *Fin de Siècle* (28 May 1892) reported that it was 'hunted down by the police' and could be used only behind closed doors; but Lautrec had been present at a gala evening at the Casino de Paris when confetti had come out of hiding.

L'Estampe Originale appeared for the first time on March 30th; it was both a magazine and a movement. Although it was revolutionary in its time, its true significance has since been underrated. Painters had been encouraged by Roger-Marx to produce engravings, especially lithographs. This brought about the decline of the printed reproduction, which had enjoyed a great vogue until then, though threatened from another direction by photography. Lautrec was one of the leading figures in this movement. Pissarro told his son about going on March 2nd to see Marty, 'who is doing a magazine of prints', and finding Lautrec there. Lautrec was occupied with a portrait of Jane Avril, a model he had been using in his painting since 1890. He treated her face in the Japanese manner, and showed her big coat which, he said, made her look like a 'coachman from the Urbaine.' The work for the magazine was done by Père Cotelle, master-printer of the Ancourt printing-works, which produced most of Lautrec's lithographs. There was a story, very much in the Lautrec manner, that Père Cotelle used the grease from his skull-cap to coat the litho stone.

Jane Avril appeared again in the poster for the Divan Japonais that came out before 30 April. It must have been she who suggested commissioning Lautrec, for the manager had already ordered a mediocre poster elsewhere to show off the interior of his place. The Divan Japonais was a rather shabby café-concert in the rue des Martyrs. It probably had that name 'because everything there is Chinese'—or rather, fake Chinese. Apparently Lautrec's wonderful poster did not help it succeed, for Arsène Alexandre wrote in July 1893 that 'it closed down before it had really opened'. People had gone there mainly to hear Yvette Guilbert, shown curiously in the poster with the top of her head cut off, as she stretches out her hands sheathed in the long black gloves that made her famous. It was no accident that Lautrec put Jane Avril into this poster with Yvette Guilbert. Jane Avril had made fun of the latter, and it was said in the popular press at the end of 1891 that people thought they had seen Yvette Guilbert at 'pleasure spots', but it was actually 'a tart who is her double, called Jane Avril'.

The poster with Jane Avril's 'black catafalque hat', as Joyant described it, was duly praised by a Socialist newspaper called *Le Père Peinard*. It congratulated Lautrec for the simplicity of his means; he was not one of those 'fools who only want to peck away at marshmallows.'

At the beginning of May, a few days after *Le Divan Japonais*, another poster appeared showing Jane Avril at the Jardin de Paris. It had much in common with *Le Divan Japonais*, and was also influenced by the work of Degas. Having started at the Moulin Rouge, Jane Avril was making her début at the Jardin de Paris following nearly two years of retirement from dancing. She may have spent that time with Lautrec. She admired him, was very fond of him, and even seems to have loved him. Lautrec too found this 'neurotic' woman attractive. He was taken by her sadness, her 'abundance of temperament' and the way she made her leg tremble while she danced 'like a delicious orchid'.

Lautrec's friends agreed with him; especially Arthur Symons, who dedicated a poem to her. Another admirer, Paul Leclercq, wrote: 'Jane Avril danced and turned, graceful, airy, a slightly crazy figure, slim, racy, weightless and flower-fed. Lautrec sang her praises.' In *Café-Concert* (1893), Montorgueil described how he was charmed by her 'tiny hint of a smile' and by 'the tip of her little slipper that poked in and out of the froth of her petticoat.' Gustave Coquiot liked 'her little rodent's face that twitched convulsively'. And in the 29 July 1893 issue of *L'Art Français*, Alexandre devoted four pages to an admiring essay on Jane Avril's dance solo, although he said that her voice was 'less practised than her legs'. He particularly praised Lautrec's poster of her: 'in three colours that are deep and clear as trumpet calls, orange, yellow and greenish-black'. The poster attracted a lot of attention and set the seal on Jane Avril's success. On 3 September *Fin de Siècle* spoke of this performer whom 'the attractive colours of Lautrec's palette have put so much in the limelight'.

Toulouse-Lautrec's 'palette' began to be well-known and admired. In March, he exhibited at the Indépendants; and on 1 April the *Chronique des Arts* put him in the first rank of artists, with Anquetin, mentioning 'his studies of peculiarly Parisian manners, which have a strange and highly individual flavour'. All this praise finally induced the Société des Indépendants to ask him to do a lithograph for its dinner menu on 23 June. Perhaps as a tribute to Degas, Lautrec drew a milliner trimming, of course, Jane Avril's hat which had so much amused him. He took great pains over this menu, both in the drawing and in the search for the right colour effects. He then had a series of 150 proofs pulled before lettering, and one printing done with lettering.

The charming milliner in this lithograph was Reneé Vert. That September she married one of Lautrec's friends, Adolphe Albert, a talented lithographer who was also secretary of the Société des Peintres-Graveurs Français. This may have had something to do with an event as important in Lautrec's life as his invitation to join the Indépendants; he was asked to take part in the fifth exhibition of that famous society of engravers. This established his reputation and showed how much he was esteemed by his contemporaries. He was invited, along with Auriol, Béjot and Duez, by the distinguished members of the society, who ranged from Redon, Buhot, Chéret and Bracquemond to Helleu and Lunois. He accepted, and sent in some proofs to show that he was working and experimenting; he also wanted to dispel the impression that he merely had a wonderful facility. The following works were submitted: the *Menu des Indépendants*, *Le Divan Japonais*, *L'Estampe Originale*, three posters, several small sketches, *La Goulue et sa sœur* (1892), *Le Petit Trottin*, and the drawing *A Saint-Lazare.*

Le Petit Trottin is the title of a sentimental ballad, a genre which Lautrec often illustrated, partly to please his composer friends, but also because their ridiculous side amused him. He called them 'sob stuff' and enjoyed singing them in his tuneless voice, just as he enjoyed collecting 'pop art'.

Joyant, who saw Lautrec at first hand, tells us the following about his technique up to 1893: the artist used Gillot paper, which made it possible to do an embossed print on zinc. It was the Goupil firm that had invented this process—also used by Daumier—in 1887. Lautrec used to experiment in charcoal, then trace the finished line, then try out colours. He deliberately made his drawing larger than the stone, either drawing on that directly or using the Gillot paper first.

In the summer of 1893, he seems to have called a halt; for some time, he did no more drawing. He retired within himself and changed enormously; and indeed, after this crisis, he showed much less interest in the finer points of the human form, or in expressive gesture. He turned, rather, to faces, especially faces highlighted by the gas-flares of the theatre. He also gave up doing posters and colour lithographs to study the technique of black and white lithography.

His interest in the human face is evident from *Vieilles Histoires*, a collection of ballads for which he produced the cover and several illustrations. The cover showed Désiré Dihau, the composer, whose songs were performed at the Chat Noir, leading a bear on a leash and going towards the Institut. The bear was Goudezki, author of the lyrics, whom Xanroff described in *Le Figaro Illustré* (1896, p. 114) as a Danubian peasant, 'a bohemian with a square head... ruddy and blond, who wore a wagoner's coat'. Dihau, who played the bassoon at the Opéra, was a friend of Lautrec's, and apparently tried to bring Degas and Lautrec together. Lautrec greatly admired Degas' portrait of Dihau.

This absorption in the human face made Lautrec's chief haunt the theatre, where he spent most of his time during the last three months of 1893. He provided theatre drawings for the newspaper *L'Escarmouche* and went to all the most popular plays and café-concert programmes. He went as readily to the Opéra as to the Moulin Rouge. His specific interest was in the expression of a face, and he would often merely sketch in the body. These newspaper drawings were afterwards produced as lithographs by Kleinmann, who had become his publisher. For some reason, this series is not well-known, although it is interesting. It portrays great actors like Bartet, Mounet-Sully, Moréno, Rose Caron, Lugné-Poë and Le Bargy. Only one of these drawings is famous—the one of Sarah Bernhardt as Phèdre—for it shows her exactly as Marcel Proust saw and described her under the name of La Berma.

This is a work of basic importance. The public had raved over Sarah Bernhardt's performance and, although she was forty-nine, this was her effective début. Jules Lemaître claimed to have 'discovered' her; this amused the press, which 'assured him that the "débutante" had been known for over twenty years in Paris and even had a world reputation'—as Arthur Meyer wrote in *Ce que je puis dire* (p. 20).

While he was working for *L'Escarmouche* or perhaps a little before, Lautrec did an album with Henri Gabriel Ibels, called *Café-Concert* (registered on 13 December), which was published under the imprint of *L'Estampe Originale*, in other words, by Marty. Lautrec's eleven lithographs were interspersed with eleven by Ibels, who was the better known of the two in those days. Ibels was considered the official painter of the *Demi-Cabots:* that is, the small-time actors in the little theatre halls where he probably took Lautrec. The two men had known each other at least since early in 1893; Lautrec had done a portrait of Ibels which was reproduced in *La Plume* on 15 January 1893. He was also the godfather of Ibels' son; he promised to make a mechanical horse for the child but, in his desire for perfection, could never finish it.

The *Café-Concert* album had an introduction by Montorgueil, a writer whose speciality was defending the cause of the players in the halls. In this introduction he maintained that 'you have to belong to your age', as Daumier had once put it; you also had to 'share in the people's entertainment' by going to the shows given in the small halls.

Lautrec's contribution to the album included portraits of Paula Brébion, of the Scala; Mary Hamilton, a *diseuse;* Edmée Lescot as a Spanish dancer; Mme Abdala; and his three favourite subjects, Bruant, Jane Avril and Yvette Guilbert. It is Guilbert's angular profile that he shows here; she looks painted in white make-up, 'deliberately pallid'. Edmond de Goncourt had extolled 'her nose, so utterly un-Grecian, and the feline glow of her eyes.' The portrait of Bruant, who was still at Les Ambassadeurs, makes an interesting comparison with the poster Lautrec had done several months earlier; there is a world of difference between the two, because Lautrec now concentrated above all on the expression of Bruant's face.

Here must be mentioned the programme for *Une Faillite*, which is dated 10 November 1893. The drawing is no better than Lautrec's other programmes of that year, but it was his first for the Théâtre Libre. This was when he began working with Antoine, leaving the world of the café-concert actors in order to concentrate on the serious, sometimes avant-garde theatre. Antoine was very fond of the play *Une Faillite*, calling it 'the most pathetic tragedy about money ever produced', but the public did not agree with him. Lautrec's drawing should be compared with the one showing Antoine and Gémier acting together, dated 1894 by Delteil.

In the spring of 1893, or by September at the latest, Lautrec drew the poster for *Au pied de l'échafaud*, a book of reminiscences written by the Abbé Faure in 1891 and serialized in the newspaper *Le Matin*. (It was later brought out in book form by the publishers Dreyfous and Dalsace.)

The Abbé Faure, who had just died at the age of sixty, had been chaplain at the prison of La Roquette and had accompanied thirty-eight men to the foot of the scaffold. Lautrec's striking poster certainly must have helped the book's sale; but those who read it were probably extremely disappointed. According to the preface, written by a Sorbonne professor called L. Crouslé, the Abbé had written 'like a good-natured and disinterested witness'—so much so that readers would 'catch themselves laughing without knowing what amused them.' The Abbé had been suspended from his post, since he had been more charitable than was wise, and had helped condemned men to communicate with the outside world. Between the composition of this poster and the *Moulin Rouge* there is a noticeable resemblance. It contains the same row of people silhouetted against the background like Chinese shadow-puppets, and the same strong patch of light—in this case, the condemned man's face. Even the executioner's hand looks like Valentin's in the earlier work.

Lautrec probably never finished reading this dull, good-natured and ironic plea, with its refrain, 'the blade swooped down and fell with a crunch on the condemned man's neck'. Yet it provided him with the inspiration for a frightening and dramatic work. It seems at first to be in complete contrast to his other works, which are bitter enough in their own way, but different in inspiration.

Maindron mentioned the poster in 1896 in the second volume of his *Affiches illustrés* (p. 112), 'The newspaper *L'Eclair*', he wrote, 'commissioned M. de Toulouse-Lautrec to do the poster for their serial *Au pied de l'échafaud*. It shows the victim's last moment: he is about to pay for his crimes. He is glazed with terror; the blood has congealed in his veins. The head, about to fall, is wonderfully observed and horribly realistic.' Joyant repeats this quotation in the second volume of his *Lautrec* (p. 114), correcting *L'Eclair* to *Le Matin*.

The poster had indeed been done for *Le Matin;* the director, Alfred Edwards, had himself comissioned it from Lautrec. Edwards kept the sketch of the poster in his office for a time, then gave it to a journalist, Félix Barbereau d'Augueville (or d'Augerville), at that time head of *Le Matin*'s information service. This man retired to Marseilles and sold the sketch to Maurice Exsteens in December 1928. The poster owes its dramatic effect to its genre as well as to its subject-matter. In those days, bookshop posters had to catch the eye with horrifying subjects; this had been the rule ever since Castelli's romantic book posters of around 1850. In an article he wrote for the *Revue des Deux-Mondes* on 'The World of Posters', Maurice Talmeyr repeated Octave Uzanne's observation that blood, murderers and crimes were needed to make people buy a book: 'walls, like Latin, defy decency'.

1894

Early in 1894, Lautrec was still working for *L'Escarmouche*. During January and February, he went on making drawings of successful plays at the new theatres, where Lugné-Poë and Antoine were acting, and also drew Marthe Brandès in her plays at the Comédie-Française. Lautrec was wonderfully skilful in interpreting the atmosphere of the Théâtre de l'Oeuvre, where the actors played in a frenzied style with their backs to the audience. The public, in fact, were very fond of innovations in acting; Jules Renard says that men wept at these performances. Lautrec also drew some unforgettable portraits of Réjane in *Madame Sans-Gêne*, and of Moréno playing Armande in *Les Femmes Savantes* 'as if she were a Botticelli'. He drew Lugné-Poë's friend Deblève in *Au-dessus des Forces Humaines*, a Scandinavian play by Bjoernstiern Bjoernson; the drawing shows the last scene, in which the husband catches his paralytic wife in his arms as she walks for the first time, then dies. He himself dies over her body; this is why Deblève is in a state of shock, his eyes cast heavenwards as his wife sinks into his arms. The actress playing the wife was Baldy.

This play startled the public and delighted some. Yet Lautrec's choice of subject is hard to understand, since he could have seen that same year a far more important play, Ibsen's *The Master Builder*.

By the time Lautrec took notice of Marthe Brandès, she had long been 'discovered'. She was already thirty-two and had begun her career in 1884. Chartran had done her portrait; but it is in Lautrec's lithographs, rather than in painted portraits or photographs, that Brandès comes to life. Her face looks highly intelligent and angular; she keeps her long, russet-coloured slit eyes half-closed. One of Lautrec's lithographs shows her in *Cabotins*, by Pailleron, playing the part of a woman of thirty-two, whose rival is a girl of eighteen. Lautrec depicts her in the studio of a sculptor, her partner in the scene being Le Bargy, whose elegance of dress and good taste apparently did little to conceal his bad acting. In another lithograph, Brandès is playing a scene with the actor Leloir in the role of her husband; they are shown arguing. This provides Lautrec with an ideal opportunity to bring out the faces and expressions of great actors—which was why he selected a play by Pailleron rather than one by Prévost or Lavedan, or *Boubouroche*, which was also showing at the time.

That same February, Lautrec executed a poster, *Babylone d'Allemagne*, for the publication of a book by one of his friends, Victor Joze, whose real name was Dobrski. A print with lettering is reproduced here, to show what the poster looked like when it papered 'every wall in Paris', as *Fin de Siècle* declared on 18 February. It was an outstanding success and gave a tremendous boost to the artist's reputation. One needs to see it without the clumsy lettering in order to form an impression of its great artistic merit. And yet, striking though it is, it clearly repeats, in reverse, the effects of the *Moulin Rouge*.

Lautrec also produced posters for two other friends; one for Sescau the photographer, the other for Marty the decorator. The Sescau poster gives the impression that the photographer used his camera to capture, at a moment in time, the beauties of Montmartre; in fact, according to Sescau's advertisements in papers like the *Grand Guignol*, he specialized in 'reproductions of paintings and enlargements of photographs'. His clients must have been puzzled by Lautrec's poster. In other respects Sescau remains a mystery. We know that he played the banjo in an amateur orchestra. Only two or three photographs can be attributed to him, one of them showing a little dog on a stool. Lautrec's poster is more daring than his previous one and recalls the experiments of the Nabi painters; it also contains both Marthe Brandès' triangular-shaped head and Yvette Guilbert's black gloves. The third poster, *L'Artisan Moderne*, is nearest to Bonnard's work; Lautrec did it for Marty's studio of popular art. This poster shows Nocq, the medallion painter, wearing a white smock; although Lautrec had painted a portrait of him, Nocq apparently disliked his work.

About this time, Lautrec also produced a colour lithograph for Les Ambassadeurs, taking Degas' *La Chanson du Chien* (1881) as his model. Lautrec and Degas cannot have been on very friendly terms, for Degas accused Lautrec quite harshly of imitating him. This was partly true. Frantz Jourdain may have had Lautrec in mind when he wrote in his interesting but forgotten book, *Les Décorés, ceux qui ne le sont pas* (1895): 'Degas showed the way to some crafty young fellows who made a fortune out of vulgarizing his methods for the philistines and watering his wine. It's easier than breeding rabbits. Degas' guests walked out of his house, taking with them the silverware and the sheets, which they use at the yearly Salon after carefully removing all the labels.'

In the same year Lautrec also produced a few more sheet-music covers; a portrait of the bicyclist, Zimmerman; and the *Menu Hébrard*, dated 26 April 1894. Adrien Hébrard was the manager of *Temps;* he was famous for his conversation and the way he made dinner parties sparkle.

From 26 April until the end of the year Lautrec's output, so prolific in 1893, was virtually confined to the album *Yvette Guilbert.*

From 5–12 May there was an exhibition of his work at the Durand-Ruel gallery. *Fin de Siècle* announced on 10 May: 'That talented and fantastical artist Toulouse-Lautrec is having an exhibition... which is highly successful. The canvasses and drawings of this witty cartoonist, so many of whose works place him in the first rank, are attracting queues of admirers.' Among the latter were painters: in an unpublished letter to Bracquemond dated 5 May Buhot announced his intention of going to the exhibition.

On 15 May, at the premises of *La Dépêche de Toulouse*, its publisher Arthur Huc, a noted enthusiast of modern art, showed some of Lautrec's works with those of sixteen other artists, including Anquetin, Bonnard, Denis, Vuillard, Vallotton and Grasset.

Lautrec's lithographic work at this time, however, was devoted to only one subject: Yvette Guilbert. He had already seen her on various occasions and drawn her once. Now he dedicated an entire album to her. It was a daring idea, for he had to obtain her agreement and be prepared to ignore the reactions of the public; for most people, not to mention the censor, would be shocked by this importance given to an individual diva.

It was probably the critic Geffroy who brought Lautrec and Yvette together. He admired both, and had been praising Lautrec's 'incisive' drawings since 1892. He therefore invited them to go boating on the Marne one summer's day. Strict propriety was observed: the two men, wearing top hats, took the oars while Yvette worked the tiller. It was a period of extreme formality in dress and Geffroy, in fact, did not decide to wear light-coloured suits during the summers until he was past sixty.

Yvette had altered her style of dress; now, in bright colours, she looked like 'an impressionist poster', according to *La Vie Parisienne* on 6 October. This amusing expression seems to prove that the singer dressed like the women-friends of the Nabi painters.

The album, containing sixteen plates and printed in an edition of one hundred copies, appeared at the beginning of August. It was first reviewed on 18 August and was registered at the Bibliothèque Nationale on 2 October. The album had a *succès de scandale;* people were indignant at this 'deification of a café-concert diva'. Yvette's family were very annoyed and her admirers thought she was 'overdone'. Goncourt received the album on 2 September; Geffroy and Frantz Jourdain went to hand it over to him personally. In an extremely disagreeable article in the *Echo de Paris* on 15 October, Jean Lorrain, who was present, recalled Goncourt's 'startled air'. 'No one has the right', Lorrain went on, 'to push the cult of ugliness so far. I know perfectly well that Mlle Guilbert is not a pretty woman, but to have agreed to the publication of these portraits is... infamous. Mlle Guilbert has been blinded by her love of publicity;

where was her feminine modesty and self-respect?... You, Yvette, accepted these drawings, which are copied from those on the walls of the Châtelet—with their murky greens and those shadows that smear your nose and chin with s—t. I came back saddened, a trifle nauseated; I felt the vague and uneasy indignation that one feels at meeting a very pretty woman on the arm of a hideous lover.'

Yvette Guilbert was shaken by the article, which matched her family's reproaches. But she let Geffroy persuade her to sign the hundred copies of the album. As for Jean Lorrain, he rarely played the prude in this way: scandal was his meat and drink. A regular reporter of the Paris scene, first launched by Léon Daudet under the name of Grenouillet, he was always at the Moulin Rouge or the race-courses, and often wrote violent pieces full of deliberate exaggeration. The other reviews, especially the one in *La Vie Parisienne*, supported Lautrec and showed no signs of outrage. Lautrec maintained that he was in earnest, that he sincerely admired Yvette, and that he found her 'captivating'. Coquiot recalls that, to prove this, Lautrec said he would 'depict her as the Diana of antiquity'. Yvette Guilbert merely laughed.

1895

In late 1894 and early 1895 Lautrec, who had always been a theatre-lover, became a stage designer himself. He did the sets for a play put on at L'Oeuvre, *Le Chariot de Terre Cuite*, by Victor Barrucand. All the young artists helped with this production. Francis Jourdain, who was eighteen then, took part, and he remembered how Lugné-Poë, always short of money, had 'made a big effort for the occasion, providing a tub full of ochred water for the supers, as the action was supposed to take place in India.'

Lugné-Poë wanted to save money. For the main set, he commissioned Lautrec, who was his friend and had previously collaborated on the sets for *Ubu*. He also suggested that the young actors should appear on stage without costumes, only draped in curtains (see his *Acrobaties*, p. 20). 'This burning but blind zeal', as Jules Lemaître described it, made the play a failure. The sets and costumes were inadequate; the audiences laughed loudly and complained. The troupe had counted heavily on the première, which was quite an occasion; all the young aesthetes wore their velvet jackets and muslin cravats, while the oval faces of their pallid women were elongated by bandeaux covering their ears.

In January 1895 Lautrec went to see Jane Avril dance at the Décadents, a café-concert at 16 *bis* rue Fontaine. He noticed an Irish singer there called May Belfort, and was immediately captivated by her face, her babyish charm, her pastel-coloured dresses and the cat she carried in her arms. May Belfort inspired one of his masterpieces, but she did not hold his attention for long. *La Revue Blanche*, Natanson, and the beautiful Missia were all making demands on his time.

He began by designing an invitation for a reception Alexandre Natanson gave at his house in the avenue du Bois de Boulogne to celebrate the unveiling of some painted decorations by Vuillard. This reception is still famous, less because of the lithographic invitation than what took place. The invitations were in English and promised 'American drinks'. These drinks happened to be just the ones Lautrec was asked to prepare; he did so, dressed as a barman, 'with inimitable skill'. Paul Leclercq saw him that evening in a white coat, wearing an American flag as a waistcoat and mixing 'solid cocktails' that promptly inebriated all the guests.

Not long afterwards, Lautrec drew the poster for the *Revue Blanche*, using as his model Missia, the wife of one of the *Revue*'s directors. But Missia posed badly; she was nervous, and was in the process of leaving her husband. Edwards, who was courting her, constantly disturbed her pose, and this made Lautrec furious. He never used her as a model again, although they remained friends. She even went to see him when he was interned in the clinic.

The *Revue Blanche* group welcomed Lautrec with open arms, especially the two humorists Tristan Bernard and Coolus. Coolus asked Lautrec to illustrate one of his tales, *Le Bézigue*, and Bernard asked him to do the cover for his *Pieds Nickelés*, which had been playing since 15 March 1894. This day was memorable for another reason: it was on 16 March that a dinner was given for which Lautrec lithographed the menu. Delteil called it *le Menu Sescau*, because it was a picture of the photographer with his banjo. The dinner may have been given in honour of *Pieds Nickelés* the day after it opened.

Lautrec kept in touch with the *Revue Blanche;* he produced some drawings for articles by Jules Renard on 15 March, and by Paul Arène and Wilde on 15 May, this last being reproduced on 2 June in *Fin de Siècle*. Thadée Natanson wrote in the *Revue* about the artist and his lithographs.

Lautrec stayed on especially friendly terms with Tristan Bernard; this enabled him to keep in touch with athletes, particularly cyclists, for Bernard was then managing the Vélodrome.

At this point Marcelle Lender entered Lautrec's life. This thirty-five-year-old actress, already plump, had made her début at the Bouffes du Nord in September 1891. After going on tour she opened again at the Variétés, on 1 February, in an operetta written during the Second Empire in the style of *La Belle Hélène*, though the action took place during the time of the Merovingians. Lender played the part of Galeswinthe and her dancing of the boléro created a sensation. Lautrec went to the play at least twenty times, just to see her. He always sat in the same seat in the first row left. The boléro reminded him of Jane Avril, Lescot, and possibly of Loie Fuller. He was absolutely enchanted with the way Lender danced, clicking her castanets, and with her way of paying compliments to the audience, singing with her hands on her hips, dancing with her back to the auditorium. 'I come just to look at Lender's back,' he used to say; 'look at it carefully—you won't see anything more wonderful.' The public agreed with him, and *La Vie Parisienne* raved about Lender's 'royal' back and 'imperial' shoulders.

Lautrec even liked the actress in street clothes and accepted Meier-Graefe's invitation to do a half-length portrait of her for the magazine *Pan*. This colour lithograph, with the wavy background in Vuillard's style, is extremely brilliant, and Lautrec mercilessly emphasized the actress's double chin in it.

Next, Lautrec drew the cast of *L'Age Difficile*, a play by Jules Lemaître. He concentrated on the beautiful Léonie Yahne, who had the part of a cyclist in the play that *La Vie Parisienne* found 'spicy'. It was about the difficult age when bachelors realize they would have done better to get married. Perhaps Lautrec thought of his own case when he saw the play, for he had felt lonely and lost when his friend, Dr Bourges, had left him to get married.

Lautrec generally drew his models full length, but his series entitled *Treize Lithographies* is of bust studies only. This album's main subjects are Jeanne Granier and Lucien Guitry. Guitry, who was thirty-five, had had a great success with his staging of Maurice Donnay's *Amants*. With that play, according to *Lucien Guitry raconté par son fils* (p. 90), 'a new name appeared in the contemporary theatre.' Jeanne Granier played opposite Guitry; Jules Renard, who saw her not long afterwards, described her in his *Journal* as 'a fresh-faced boy, with curly red hair. Her deep voice sounds as though she has a cold. "I'm no actress," she claims. "I just play that way."'

The album also contains several drawings of Jeanne Hading, a thirty-six-year-old actress who was playing with great success in *Les Demi-Vierges* at the Gymnase. Catulle Mendès described her acting and her beauty in lyrical terms. He related how, in a school near London (she had toured both the United States and England once), there was a photograph of her in every dormitory. 'Those children were right', Mendès wrote, 'to see in her an image of incomparable loveliness.'

The same album includes a portrait presumed to be of Sarah Bernhardt, one of Polin, and one, or perhaps several, of Polaire. It is an uneven series, wrongly neglected by art historians because it is very rare. Firm, precise drawings are grouped alongside barely discernible figures, some of which are rather poor.

1895 was the year of Lautrec's triumph; he had his admirers, his supporters and his publishers. Let us quote three significant texts:

In his *Carnavals parisiens* (p. 46), Morin said: 'There is actual derisive laughter instead of mere illusion in Lautrec's expression of the grotesque.' Maindron wrote in *La Plume* on 15 November: 'M. de Toulouse-Lautrec is less widely known than Chéret, yet he deserves better. His dominant characteristic is boldness. Not everyone has seen the things he paints, and what he paints is not alluring; but that is not his main concern. He goes his own way and finds approaches to the public by unexpected means. He has really worked to improve his draughtsmanship and he brings to the world of posters and painting a talent which is clearly *impressionistic*... He uses a new language; but this language is firm and clear, with a harmony of its own. It will be understood, for all his works are genuinely important.' In *Les Décorés, ceux qui ne le sont pas* (p. 209, 212, 213), Frantz Jourdain exclaimed: 'Well, well! Here's one who isn't bored with life... He's known to all gay Paris, this assiduous habitué of the Moulin Rouge, the Casino, the

Folies-Bergère, the Montmartre brasseries, the eccentric cafés and the vulgar music-halls. He's the wandering Jew of wedding-feasts and parties. More than that, he's highly intellectual and cultivated; an artist of taste from the highest level of society... His works have a striking air of mournful sadness... He mixes cocktails with a dexterous flourish and a sense of perfection that the most famous barman in the United States would envy... He's a fantastic satirist because he doesn't distort nature, he just waits until her grotesque form is revealed.'

According to *Art Moderne* on 21 February, the Salon des Vingt at Brussels was 'by unanimous opinion the most important exhibition of modern art ever held in Belgium.' Lautrec sent in *The Fair Miss H.*, *Cissy Loftus*, various lithographs, posters (*Le Pendu* and *Confetti*), as well as a selection of prints from *L'Estampe Originale*.

In 1895 Lautrec was also invited to take part in a large national exhibition of art in honour of the centenary of lithography, which took place in Paris. He submitted *La Goulue et sa sœur*, *La Loge au mascaron doré*, and *Leloir et Brandès* (two large colour lithographs and one in black and white).

Now that he was known and appreciated, Lautrec took the failure of his *Napoléon* very badly. Boussod and Valadon had organized a contest for a poster to announce a biography of Napoleon written in English for the American market. Boussod, Lautrec's publisher, asked the artist to enter the competition, convinced that he would win. But Frédéric Masson, a Napoleonic historian, and the painters who sat on the jury, Detaille, Gérome and Vibert, selected the unknown Métivet, a friend of Lautrec's youth, who was often photographed by his side. Masson refused to buy Lautrec's sketch for 200 francs, and the painter decided to have the poster printed in an edition of one hundred at his own expense.

1896

Two trials stirred public opinion during 1896. The first was the Lebaudy case, the second was the trial of Arton.

Lautrec caught the essence of the Lebaudy case in his lithograph of Mlle Marsy in the witness box. An actress of the Comédie-Française, she gave evidence for the defence in the case which followed Lebaudy's death. She caused a sensation with her large, black-feathered hat and her general elegance, which Lautrec showed off skilfully against the lawyers in their caps and the municipal police. She had been the mistress of Lebaudy, who was known as 'Little Sugar-bowl' because of his family's vast sugar refineries. Mlle Marsy had nursed him when he fell ill during his unwilling military service. The rather shady Lebaudy affair helped to discredit the bourgeoisie even more than the Dreyfus case. Lautrec did not publish this plate, though he had a few copies printed.

But he did publish the three plates he drew that April of the Arton trial. The first, mistitled *Déposition*

Dupas by Delteil, actually shows Arton speaking in his own defence. Léopold Aaron, alias Arton, had been accused of corrupting parliament over the Panama affair. The Baron de Reinach had reportedly given him one and a half million francs to distribute among various deputies. Arton had been sentenced *in absentia* to serve five years in prison and to pay a heavy fine, but for three years, with police connivance, he had avoided arrest. When finally caught he went on trial and was acquitted, but the public had no illusions about the real nature of the case.

Lautrec's second plate showed Alexandre Ribot making a statement that he had given the order for Arton's arrest on 13 January 1893, while he was Keeper of the Seals. His fine face and his air of loyalty made an impression on Lautrec as well as the public. Ribot's features form a contrast with the clownish look of the audience. In the third plate the Inspector-General of the Sûreté, Soudais, is shown giving evidence. This 'fat, jovial fellow, with his ruddy cheeks and good-natured air of a retired sergeant spinning yarns over a pint at the bar, is giving racy accounts of his man-hunt through Europe,' reported *L'Illustration* on 28 March.

Arton is said to have been delighted by Lautrec's lithographs. The story goes that he hung one up in his toilet to bolster his courage every morning, 'for he was certainly not the most embarrassed man in these historic sessions', as Coquiot wrote in the work already cited (p. 163).

Lautrec's other lithographs of 1895 include bar scenes and cyclists. He also executed several posters, programmes and menus. His fame had spread; a Chicago ink-manufacturer named Wiborg commissioned one of the posters. Let us examine a few works from this exceptional period; first, a programme for the stage production at L'Oeuvre on 10 February, a particularly important occasion when both Romain Coolus' *Raphaël* and Oscar Wilde's *Salome* were presented. Lugné-Poë had commissioned the programme-lithograph and he was delighted with it. *Salome* was a success. Wilde was in prison at the time, and the *Echo de Paris* reported that the applause of the first-night audience 'rang across the Channel, through the English prison-walls, to reach the unfortunate prisoner in Reading Gaol.' This pleased Lautrec; although he was in no way attracted to Wilde, he felt that the sentence was much too harsh, as did his friends the Natansons. He also illustrated an article on the defence of Wilde, written by Henri de Régnier for the *Revue Blanche* in 1895. Lautrec's portrait was made at the trial, which he attended; Wilde had refused to pose.

Another important work, dated 1896, is the poster of Mlle Eglantine's troupe which was about to leave on tour. The fast and furious days of La Goulue and the Moulin Rouge were over. The French can-can had become infinitely genteel; Montorgueil says that the English found Mlle Eglantine's girls far too respectable. Mistinguett remembered seeing, in her youth, this Lautrec poster on the walls of Paris when she herself was making her début at the Trianon Lyrique: 'There was a poster by Toulouse-Lautrec which showed Jane Avril's legs, dancing the can-can in Mlle Eglantine's troupe... The public, in fact, preferred Chéret to Toulouse-Lautrec; Chéret used to drew provocative little ladies. There was Mucha too, and his "modern style"... Perhaps the posters are what I remember best and looked at the most.' Lautrec's posters, of which this was nearly his last, may not have made an impression on everyone who saw them, but young artists appreciated them extremely. Picasso had one in his Montmartre studio, and Braque recalls how, when he was very young at Le Havre, he used to watch from his window while the bill-sticker papered the wall opposite with posters signed by Lautrec; as soon as the man had finished his work, the boy would leap out, unglue the fresh poster, and use it to paper the walls of his room.

For present-day collectors and historians of lithography, 1896 is above all the year of *Elles*.

The subject of *Elles* is life in brothels. Lautrec wanted to show that their inmates were not damned, but lived like everybody else. He had got to know these women well, especially during the previous two years, and he called them *Elles* because this was, at the time, a term used for women in general. Except for the first lithograph and the penultimate one, there is nothing to show that these are not ordinary women making an honest living. This was not a wholly new approach. Proust had noted the same state of affairs with astonishment; after dreaming, like des Esseintes, of 'caresses in a false atmosphere of macabre perversity', he discovered that the girls in the brothel he visited held 'long conversations' with him and offered him camomile tea. All Lautrec's circle were convinced, as he was, that 'tarts' had 'exquisite feelings, unknown to virtuous women'. There was no similarity between this series and the facile eroticism of Lautrec's two contemporaries, Boutet (*Levers et couchers des Parisiennes*, 1896) and Pal (*L'Amour dans ses meubles*).

This album of ten lithographs and a cover marks a peak in Lautrec's art. He used three models: the first was the youthful Pauline, known as Mlle Popo, whom Paul Guilbert claimed to have kept. Pauline lived with her mother, the fearsome Mme Baron, who also posed, dressed in her chemise. The third was a big woman, mainly seen washing herself.

The series shows Vuillard's influence, but its chief interest lies in the outstanding mastery of Lautrec himself. It was not successful. Pellet was unable to sell the hundred copies that were printed, though he found it easy enough to sell pale imitations of Degas and Lautrec by Legrand. Yet artists took notice. *Fin de Siècle's* use of the world *Elles*, in its issue of 23 July 1892, to describe that type of woman was exceptional, but it was adopted by the painter Truchet as the title for one of his paintings, exhibited at the Salon of 1889. This painting showed a group of women, wearing long dresses, in an indoor setting.

An art magazine called *L'Aube*, for which Lautrec had once drawn a poster, spoke highly of his series. It stressed Lautrec's special status and 'intense' personality; it spoke of his work as being 'very skilful, less crude than at the start.' It specifically mentioned the woman done in sepia, and the woman at her toilette. *La Plume*, the *Courrier Français*, *La Justice* and the *Revue Blanche* also praised the series, and Vollard had it exhibited in 1897 after its presentation at the Salon des Cent in 1896.

That year, Lautrec exhibited as usual at the Brussels Libre Esthétique as well; but this time he sent in only posters—those of May Milton, of May Belfort (before lettering), of *La Revue Blanche*, and of the *Salon des Cent*, better known as *La Passagère*. An article written by A. Joly in *Libre Critique* on 29 March praised the vigour, the charm and the delicate tones of the master's posters.

In April, Lautrec's lithographs were again exhibited at Joyant's gallery in Paris; Goncourt, who had been invited, wrote in his diary on 20 April: 'Exhibition of lithographs by Lautrec, a dwarf of a man. All his drawings seem to reflect his own caricature-like deformity.' Goncourt was not the only one to find a connection between the man and his works. Two years later, Alexandre Hepp wrote: 'The odd, deformed and limping man was evident in the works, which is something rare. Many of his startling subjects had his own traits and appearance, as though he were obsessed with them. His looks had an influence on his work, and in the strangest fashion, again and again, the artist's body seemed to bear down on his personality in a direct and bitter way, as if he lacked a soul to set him free.'

Lautrec dedicated a copy of a dinner menu of 29 December to Pellet, his 'dauntless publisher'. Although he was not selling any copies of *Elles*, Pellet commissioned several colour lithographs from Lautrec, which came out between January and July 1897.

Lautrec was feeling weary. Joyant advised him to resuscitate his old themes, such as the Moulin Rouge and the theatre. And so, still with great talent, Lautrec drew *La Grande Loge*, *La Petite Loge*, and *L'Idylle Princière*, three studies of an audience's behaviour and appearance during a show. He also drew *La Clownesse* from *Elles* (Cha-U-Kao, done as a painting in 1895), and *Les Deux Amies au Moulin Rouge* (a painting subject in 1892). Finally he drew *Elsa la Viennoise*, who was supposed to be one of the girls at the house in the rue des Moulins. Between twelve and twenty-five copies only were made of these prints.

1897

In 1897 Lautrec illustrated a book by Clemenceau called *Au pied du Sinaï*. No one has yet established the means by which this came about, but Clemenceau's publisher, Floury, was a friend of Marty, who later published the *Histoires naturelles*. And Clemenceau's sub-editor at *La Justice*, and afterwards at *L'Aurore*, was the critic Gustave Geffroy, the friend of Lautrec who had arranged his meeting with Yvette Guilbert. So it is not difficult to see why Lautrec might have been selected for the job. He found the Jewish physiques he drew for the book so interesting that he slipped many other Semitic profiles into the illustrations he produced at that time.

Another publisher, Vollard, asked Lautrec to produce a colour lithograph for his album of painter-engravers, which came out in 1897. This was *La Charrette anglaise*, a drawing of the dog-carts that were so typical of the time, built of 'teak, with nickel-plated iron work that shone like razor-blades' (J. Lorrain, *Fards et poisons*). It is a bold piece, with simplified lines and bright contrasts. It is also one of Lautrec's last lithographs in colour.

Perhaps an article by Thiébault-Sisson in *Temps* (1897) gave him a shock. In it, colour lithography was branded as 'a deplorable habit' which 'annoyed and maltreated the eye'. Colour was decreed suitable only for posters; lithography had to revert to black and white, even in the case of Lautrec, who 'venerates the album of Yohivara d'Outamaro'. On 22 January 1898, in a report to the president of the engraving and lithography section of the Artistes Français, Henri Lefort also said that engravings in colour were nothing but cheap illustrations; 'by origin, by tradition and by basic principle, engraving is undeniably an art of the black and white.'

Even Lautrec's posters became open to criticism. Lucien Muhfeld, in *L'Affichage moderne*, accused them of not advertising anything. As an example he took the poster for the *Revue Blanche:* one could, of course, see 'an insignificant-looking woman, slender, well-built and very elegant', but this would not induce anyone to buy a magazine of art and literature. Therefore, Lautrec's posters were 'commercially useless'. The verdict was 'high quality as art, inferior as posters'.

Criticism made Lautrec uneasy and restless. He moved from his studio in the rue Tourlaque to another in the avenue Frochot. On 15 May he gave a house-warming party, inviting his friends to have a glass of milk with him: the invitation cards showed him with a cow. He did in fact serve milk and strawberries, while a barman mixed cocktails in a corner. This must have been one of his jokes, for a milk-bar, called La Laiterie des Pins, had recently opened in Paris. Willette had designed its invitations, and it had immediately become very fashionable. But papers like the *Courrier Français*, *Le Matin* and *Le Journal* wrote satirical comments on it and printed cartoons showing a waiter asking a client if he would have 'a drop of his usual milk'. Hermann Paul particularly made puns on the words *lait* and *laid*. This point needs to be emphasized because the invitation cards used to be dated 1900 and were thought to show that Lautrec was mentally disturbed. Actually it was only meant as an ironic joke, which was shared by a whole group of caricaturists.

The wholesome pleasures of milk were not Lautrec's only joys. He began going to the bars of Montmartre more and more often. His two favourites were Le Hanneton and La Souris, both of them frequented only by women. Lautrec had always been interested in Lesbians, and he drew a great many, starting with La Goulue in 1892. His was the curiosity of a man who liked women and normal love. He now became a regular at Le Hanneton, a bar run by Mme Brazier, whom he depicted in his lithograph *La Grande Loge*. But he seems to have preferred La Souris or 'La Touris', as he used to call it, run by Mme Armande Palmyre. Lapparent describes seeing Lautrec there 'under the crude glare of the electric lights, surrounded by a dozen fleshy women, all wearing severe mens' jackets and starched collars'. Lautrec certainly met Bottini there, who had come to him for inspiration. Palmyre's obese gravity amused Lautrec; he used to say that 'with her heart on her sleeve, she looks as if she wants to gobble everything up'. That June, Lautrec did a portrait of Mme Palmyre at La Souris. He also drew her bulldog at the top of a menu.

Lautrec always loved animals, especially horses and dogs. It was this which had attracted him to Jules Renard. Naturally, he was also a great admirer of *Poil de carotte*. At Lautrec's wish, the two men had met on 26 November 1894, and Renard wrote in his diary: 'He's a tiny little blacksmith who wears pince-nez, a shapeless little carpet-bag of a man. He has thick lips, and his hands are like the ones he draws, with splayed bony fingers and curved thumbs... At first, his smallness pains you, but then you notice that he's very lively and extremely nice. He grunts between sentences, and this makes his lips part, the way the wind lifts the padding around the edge of a door.'

The two men became quite friendly. Early in 1895, Lautrec did some studies for a fox's head which was to be incorporated in an ornamented letter at the head of an article by Renard for the *Revue Blanche*. On 16 December 1895 Lautrec made Renard a formal offer, asking to illustrate about eight of the author's *Histoires naturelles*, in an edition of a hundred copies to be sold at approximately 25 francs each. Renard accepted; but the scheme took a long time to reach completion.

During 1896 and 1897 Lautrec spent a good deal of time drawing animals. He went regularly to the Jardin des Plantes and used to take his friends there. During this period, he also collected the strangest animals, giving them away in 1900 to various decorators as models. Renard was pleased, and occasionally delighted, with some of the drawings; of one, he said, 'There's a pig that's already sausage meat.' But basically the two men did not see eye to eye. Lautrec regretted the fact that Renard has chosen the most ordinary animals: 'Surely the donkey, the dog, the horse and the rooster aren't everything.' For this reason, perhaps, Renard went to the zoo himself; his visits provided him with some new epithets, such as 'the llama smiles like Sarah Bernhardt; the kangaroo walks on its calves...' But this did not speed up work on the book, which suffered several interruptions, and it did not come out until early in 1899.

1898

In 1898, after trying out drypoint for portraits of his friends, Lautrec used lithography, in his private work, only to draw a man who hired out carriages, the man's horses and especially his dog.

But he received several commissions. The Boussod and Manzi firm asked him for another portrait of Marcelle Lender printed in brown on blue paper; it was Joyant, in fact, who ran the Paris branch of Boussod. The London gallery that held a one-man show of Lautrec's works that year also belonged to the Boussod firm. The Lender portrait that Lautrec did for them is very handsome, but lacks the dash and vigour of those of 1895; it is a bit insipid and too proper. Lautrec felt no need to see the actress again for this portrait; he merely had another look at his previous drawings, and perhaps used an old sketch as a basis.

Another commission came from the English publishers, Bliss and Sands, who asked him to do an album of eight lithographs of Yvette Guilbert. Once again Lautrec did not have to go and see his model, for she sang the same songs as in 1895 and still wore the same long black gloves. But this time Lautrec concentrated on her profile with its turned-up nose 'that would be so convenient', as Jules Renard once said, 'if one felt like kissing her'. Broadly conceived, the plates in this splendid volume are done in light feathery strokes that must often have barely touched the stone—a technique that may have disappointed the public, but was not so different from Whistler's. For this year, Joyant also speaks of a project for a poster for 'Job', a cigarette paper, and of experimental sketches for the cover of a book called *Le Fauconnier*.

The rest of Lautrec's output in 1898 was done for his own satisfaction, for the sheer pleasure of working. He experimented on copper and made some drawings at Stern's printing shop, dedicating the few copies of these prints to the proprietor.

Lautrec was 'tempted to work in drypoint', Francis Jourdain wrote in *Né en 76*; 'on my advice, he is going to have a thin sheet of zinc cut for him at an ironmonger's in the rue des Martyrs, who is well-known to beginners and freelancers, but despised by professional engravers... Lautrec scratches away at his piece of zinc with a blunt steel point.' Lautrec dedicated the first of nine plates to his neighbour, Robin. These consist of a series of portraits of friends, some of which are not yet properly identified; all, however, are of excellent quality, especially the ones of Tristan Bernard and Francis Jourdain. The latter once met Lautrec at the printer Delâtre's, when the artist was bringing in the portrait of Charles Maurin: '"What's good about this portrait", he said, "is that it looks very much like something by William Morris"; he then gave me a copy which he dedicated on the back.' This joke shows Lautrec's timidity; he could not admit to a young friend that he had succeeded in anything.

The drypoint etchings were done at the beginning of the year. The lithographs of the dogs and the horses cannot be dated exactly, as Lautrec went to London for some time during that Spring. They have all been grouped together in our illustrations, although Delteil spread them out over the years 1898 to 1901, because they do have a common ingredient: a funny little black dog with upright ears and a curled tail, which might be a bull-terrier. This dog appears on the cover of *L'Etoile Rouge*, which came out in 1898; it can also be found in lithographs with Edmond Calmèse, who kept a livery stable at 10 rue Fontaine. Lautrec cultivated Calmèse because of his carriages and his horses, especially one pony called Philibert. 'It was a tiny animal on rickety legs, pot-bellied and gimlet-eyed,' Leclerq wrote. 'Philibert had become a personality for Lautrec. He insisted I had to make its acquaintance and spoke of it as a friend... not a day went by without his going to the stables to give Philibert some sugar.' Lautrec did indeed produce many drawings of this pony.

The little dog appears again in a woman's bed; also at the side of the strange-eyed Lesbian from La Hanneton, one of Lautrec's best lithographs of that year (it was registered in November 1898); and in the background of a motoring scene.

Two of Lautrec's 1898 lithographs were technically different from the rest. Usually, he achieved his effects in a few strokes; but in his portrait of Adolphe Albert and in *Le Vieux Cheval*, he drew in a detailed manner and used heavy shading. This unusual technique was not repeated. Was he trying to please his friend Albert? No one knows.

Lautrec's condition had grown serious, and he became gravely unbalanced that winter. He was hardly working any longer. Joyant may have given him some commissions specifically to help him pull himself together, to turn towards the past and forget the present.

It was at this time that Lautrec, who had become increasingly well-known around Montmartre, was used as a character in a novel by Hugues Rebell, *La Câlineuse*, which came out in 1899.

Lautrec was represented by the character called Jacques de Tavannes, who was small, like Lautrec, and 'leaned upon his little cane, bent double and seeming even tinier.' Like Lautrec, whose clothes were too light in colour, Tavannes dressed 'like a jester'. He would 'lift his short legs, rub his hands together, turn from left to right, and never keep still. His close-shaven head was huge on his little body, and his face disappeared behind a thick black beard that he seemed to have grown on purpose to hide his comic, faun-like features.' Just like Lautrec, who went everywhere with his tall cousin, Tavannes would go about with a giant, 'lifting up his nose while the other bent over'. Tavannes painted 'mysteriously ugly' subjects, revealed new aspects of them, and turned his models into 'hallucinations'. His friends compared him to Goya, to Steen, to Japanese artists. His studio, like Lautrec's, was 'half temple, half bazaar', littered with every kind of object: weapons, silks, chipped chinaware and dolls. This novel even has an anecdote very much in Lautrec's style, though his biographers have not mentioned it. Tavannes hires the Moulin de la Galette to give a *bal des jolies rencontres*. Then, climbing up on to a stool, he explains 'in his drawling, bantering voice that he had wanted to confront virtuous women with prostitutes, that is to say, the most respected members of one of our most useful professions.'

Having thus been turned into a fictional character, Lautrec's artistic limitations began to be noticed by some, including his own publisher Manzi, Joyant's partner. Joyant's open admiration for Lautrec may have exasperated Manzi a little; when Albert Flament met him in October 1898, and called Lautrec an 'explorer of the bawdy-houses' who had opened up new fields of vision and delineation, Manzi replied that Lautrec had been 'pricked off' by Degas. Flament adds (in *Bal du Pré-Catalan*) that Manzi put 'such subtlety into the way he said the word "pricked" that it gave me a thrill of pleasure.' It was probably late in 1898 that Lautrec drew *Le Promenoir*, which was included in Meier-Graefe's album *Germinal*, dated 1899. Again he drew from memory, evoking figures from the past, particularly one round-faced woman who had been his model in his brothel phase.

1899–1900

Lautrec's condition grew worse at the beginning of 1899. His canvasses were stacked away in his studio, and he hardly worked at all. He did produce a poster for an old friend, Jane Avril, which he dated 1899; but it was never used. Historians used to look on it as the work of a madman, but it is now recognized as a typical work of 1900, in line with the sort of experiment he was doing that year.

Other works of this period, however, certainly have a mad, obsessive and erotic quality, particularly *Le Chien et le perroquet*, which he dated 8 February 1899. His mother had left him, and most of his friends had given him up in despair of his drunkenness and instability. For nearly the entire month of January 1899, he wandered around the bars and the wine-sellers with Calmèse, who by this time had become his evil genius. On 17 March he was confined in Dr Sémelaigne's clinic, where he stayed until 20 May.

After an alcoholic cure, he pulled himself together almost immediately. Out of pride, he wanted to prove that he was sane. There was only one way: to work and to show his works. 'My drawings bought me my freedom,' he said.

Paint-brushes, pencils, canvasses and stones were brought to him. He began to go out again, visited the zoo, and finished the illustrations for Renard's *Histoires naturelles*, which he had begun several years earlier. The printer Stern saw him doing two animal drawings from memory. His monotypes of a male and female clown, also done from memory, probably date from this time as well.

He left the clinic on 20 May, and on 3 June the *Echo de Paris* announced his 'complete recovery, which will delight all the admirers of this excellent artist.' Joyant took him travelling to Le Crotoy, Le Havre, and Taussat; he returned to Paris in the autumn.

On his return, Lautrec took up lithography again. He drew *L'Anglaise du 'Star'*, a bar in Le Havre which had caught his fancy that summer, and a few other works. Nicholson was right to see a new sense of construction emerging in these lithographs, attributable, perhaps, to Cézanne's canvasses, which he could have seen at Vollard's.

Lautrec then executed a series on the world of race-courses. The choice of this theme may have been dictated by Pierrefort, the publisher from the rue Bonaparte who produced the famous colour lithograph *Le Galop d'essai*, usually called *Le Jockey*. This was one of the few times Lautrec handled the subject, and he seems to have been rarely visiting the races at that time. Another work of this period was *Le Jockey se rendant au poteau*, also in colour. On 8 May 1902, Lotz wrote on a copy of this work: 'Lautrec's last lithograph, unfinished.'

In January 1900 came the poster of *La Gitane* for Marthe Mellot; in April, *La Modiste* or *Mme Le Margouin*, for Joyant; and not long afterwards a cover for Paul Leclerq. *La Modiste* is the best of these final works; it may have been done in 1899—the date Joyant gives for a profile drawing of 'Mme Le

Margouin'—and may be Lautrec's last work. For more and more, in his last years, he turned from lithographs to drawings. He drew the cover for the *Album d'images animées*, *Le Motographe*; and another of his drawings was reproduced as a poster for the Bal des Etudiants in 1900 at Bordeaux. He produced sketches for sheet-music covers, notably the one for Dihau's ballad, *Tes Yeux*.

In any case, his work was almost at a standstill. Joyant claims that, from the end of 1899 until May 1900, and from 15 April to 15 July 1901, Lautrec went to the bois de Boulogne every day to look at the horses. All he would talk about with Frantz Toussaint, who met him in April 1900, was horses. Yet the period 1899–1900 saw the creation of several outstanding works of unprecedented vigour.

He was now so famous that he was asked to be a member of the jury of the lithography section of the Exhibition of 1900. He refused, knowing that he did not share the officials' rather narrow tastes.

He may not have been working but he continued to see his young friends, who learned to draw from him and would be his successors. He found this a source of satisfaction and said to one of them, Capiello: 'We were like two dogs sniffing at each other; we had to meet.'

PATRONS AND PUBLIC

It is very difficult to analyze the public of a poster artist. But various witnesses from Mistinguett to Braque prove that people who saw them in the street found Lautrec's posters extremely striking. His were among the first to be detached from walls and bought from bill-stickers. It was largely due to Lautrec that people started collecting posters towards 1900, in spite of the difficulty of preserving them.

Lautrec did not have the same public for his lithographs. They were not less appreciative, but they were satisfied to own his works in the form of sheet-music covers or newspaper-pages. Collectors hardly bought the special editions limited to forty, sixty or a hundred prints, for their benefit. And yet, these prints were done with care, Lautrec supervising each printing to check on its quality and its number. 'When he did a lithograph,' said Paul Leclerq, 'he would draw without erasure directly onto the stone. He would then take the stone to a craftsman called Stern, who did the actual printing in Lautrec's presence. Lautrec examined the prints, one by one, as they came out of the press. He tore up the ones which did not satisfy him... When the printing was finished, he smeared the stone in such a way that it could never be used again, and, to stop all fraud, he made an individual and imperceptible mark on each copy of a limited edition.' But the big collectors of prints had other preferences, usually engravings, and the small collectors found the special editions too expensive.

The firm of Boussod published Lautrec's colour lithographs from 1892. It was a powerful firm, dealing exclusively in lithographs and in coloured pictures which were extremely saleable. In 1888 'His Excellency M. Boussod', as Van Gogh called him, went into partnership with Manzi and Maurice Joyant, Lautrec's friend. Joyant thus became Lautrec's first publisher and was to commission more works from the artist.

Lautrec's first posters were commissioned by the show directors Zidler and Ducarre, even though Ducarre refused to pay for the poster of Bruant.

After 1893, Lautrec was backed by André Marty, the 'modern style' publisher and decorator who founded *L'Artisan Moderne* and published the albums of *L'Estampe Originale*. He also published the albums *Café-Concert* and *Yvette Guilbert* (1894).

Lautrec worked for song publishers from at least 1887, especially for Ondet who lived in the same house as his printer, Ancourt, at 83 rue du Faubourg-Saint-Denis. Ondet, who published the songs of Lautrec's friend Dihau, produced a commercial edition of Lautrecs, using the original lithographs that had been printed in editions of ten to a hundred copies. Georges Darien, publisher of *L'Escarmouche*, did the same thing in 1893–1894; he printed editions of one hundred from the stones and then had electrotypes made for his newspaper.

After November 1893, Lautrec had a new publisher in the rue de la Victoire, called Kleinmann, who brought out his lithographs of actors and actresses between 1894 and 1896. Yet Kleinmann seems to have acted only as an agent, for Lautrec reserved the right of asking him to send copies of his works to critics and various other people.

In 1896 and 1897 Lautrec's publisher was Gustave Pellet. At that time thirty-seven years old, son of a bankrupt family, Pellet had become a publisher of prints and a bookseller on the quai Voltaire, making a start by selling off his private collection of books. At the end of 1895, Goncourt noted in his diary: 'Pelet [sic], the quai Voltaire publisher, looks like a medieval torturer, and is always accompanied by his two big dogs.' Pellet, who was interested in eroticism, published Louis Legrand (300 plates), Rops (400), Maurin (100) and Lautrec (80). Lautrec became attached to Pellet, who was also friendly with Anquetin and Grenier. Important Pellet publications were *Elles* in 1890, and *La Clownesse* and *Elsa la Viennoise* in 1897.

Pierrefort, a young publisher in the rue Bonaparte, projected a series on the races, but only *Le Jockey* came out (in 1899). This lithograph was printed after Lautrec's confinement at Neuilly, and Stern brought Pierrefort to the clinic on 17 May.

Lautrec's lithographs also had a following abroad. In 1895 a German magazine called *Pan*, edited in France by Meier-Graefe, commissioned the colour lithograph of Marcelle Lender. Meier-Graefe, a historian and admirer of impressionism, was called a 'Francophobe' by J. E. Blanche. In Paris he worked with Bing, the decorator: both were involved with the Art Nouveau movement. Lautrec took part in the first Salon of Art Nouveau, at Bing's premises, on 26 December 1895. In 1896, the American ink manufacturer Wiborg commissioned him to do a poster, just as the Englishman Bella had ordered *Confetti*. Other Englishmen commissioned a few plates and two series, *Treize Lithographies* and the second Yvette Guilbert album.

Yet it is hard to identify all his prints. He very rarely dedicated them, except to his models and to critics like Deschamps, the director of *La Plume*. Stern did ask him for a dedicated copy of each print he struck, but neither Ancourt, Père Cotelle nor Chaix made this request. The copies dedicated to Stern are mainly works of 1898–1899, although there is one dated 1896.

Thanks to the notes of Edmond Sagot, the big Parisian dealer in modern prints, we get a clearer picture of Lautrec's clientèle on the eve of his death. The first striking thing is Sagot's own position. He was extremely interested in Lautrec and began collecting the artist's work as early as 1900, though his principal acquisitions were made in 1902 from Manzi and Stern. In 1901 Sagot sold some to Jalby, Beraldi, Marcel Guérin, Mutiaux, Matheus and Lotz. Matheus sold his Lautrecs in 1911, Lotz in 1919. Outside of these, two important collections were those of Roger-Marx, which was sold in 1914, and Pochet, whose sale in 1902 created such a stir that M. Paul Prouté still remembers it.

Eugène Mutiaux was one of the most interesting collectors of that period. As Guérin put it, his taste was 'very subtle and very sure'. He had collected nearly all the graphic works of Lautrec and used to predict that some day Lautrec's drawings and prints would be prized like the works of Watteau. 'But few collectors agreed with this,' Guérin recalls. 'One day, in a fit of disgust, Groult pretended to tear up my copy of *Blanche et Noire*... "Oh, that arm!" he roared, "that arm..." Youth and passion made me see red; I found it difficult to conceal my anger. I had bought that print for 15 francs and I already saw it as a masterpiece.'

After Lautrec's death, Guérin and Mutiaux went on adding to their collections, which grew larger and larger. New collectors appeared: Barrion (whose collection was sold in 1906), Georges Viau, Henraux (sold in 1910), Gerstenberg (sold in 1908) and Doucet. Museums began to take an interest: the Budapest Museum assembled a collection by buying from Sagot in 1912; the Stockholm Museum made some purchases in 1908; the Copenhagen Museum had acquired posters before 1900 and Seidlitz bought some for Munich. A Lautrec print fetched from 50 to 60 francs between 1902 and 1912. The separate printings from *Le Rire*, supplied by Kleinmann and Blaizot, were priced at 1.50 francs apiece. The posters cost 3.50 with lettering, 10 (and soon 50) francs before lettering. The famous photographer, Steichen, bought some Lautrecs in 1909. On 14 February 1902 the Comtesse de Toulouse-Lautrec presented the Cabinet des Estampes in Paris with 371 lithographs in memory of her son: proofs, successive printings and entire series, carefully selected for her in Joyant's printing works.

After the First World War, the print-rooms at most of the important museums formed collections of Lautrec; there were many purchases after 1920 by Stockholm, The Hague (1922), the Albertina in Vienna (1923), Dresden, Boston (1924), the Chicago Art Institute (1932), Baltimore and others. Claude Roger-Marx, Maurice Loncle, Atherton Curtis and Oprescu all built up collections. Everywhere, Lautrec had become recognized as a master.

BIBLIOGRAPHY

Bouret, Jean, *Toulouse-Lautrec*, London, 1964

Delteil, Loÿs, *Le Peintre-Graveur Illustré* (Vols. x and xi). (First illustrated catalogue of prints), Paris, 1920

Guérin, Marcel, *Toulouse-Lautrec, Lithographies*, Paris, 1948

Huisman, Philippe and Dortu, M. G., *Lautrec par Lautrec*, Lausanne and Paris, 1964

Jedlicka, Gotthard, *Henri de Toulouse-Lautrec*, Berlin, 1929 (Zürich, 1943)

Jourdain, Francis and Adhémar, Jean, *Toulouse-Lautrec*, Paris, 1952

Joyant, Maurice, *Henri de Toulouse-Lautrec* (Vol. i: catalogue of paintings and drawings; Vol. ii: lithographs and engravings), Paris, 1926–27

Julien, Edouard, *Les Affiches de Lautrec*, Monte Carlo, 1950

Mack, Gerstle, *Toulouse-Lautrec*, New York, 1938

Nicholson, B., 'Notes on Toulouse-Lautrec', *Burlington Magazine*, September 1951

Perruchot, Henri, *La Vie de Toulouse-Lautrec*, Paris, 1958

Pérusseaux, Charles, 'Suivre Lautrec dans la création d'une lithographie', *Les Lettres Françaises*, 17 February 1955

Roger-Marx, Claude, *The Lithographs of Toulouse-Lautrec*, London and Paris, 1948

Catalogue of Toulouse-Lautrec's graphic work at the Bibliothèque Nationale, by Jean Adhémar, introduction by J. Vallery-Radot, preface by Julien Cain, Paris, 1951

PLATES

MOULIN ROUGE
MOULIN ROUGE
MOULIN ROUGE
CONCERT
BAL
TOUS LES SOIRS
LA GOULUE
HLautrec
AFFICHES AMÉRICAINES CH LEVY 10 Rue Martel PARIS

1

4

ELDORADO

aristide BRUANT dans soncabaret

Imp. BOURGERIE & Cie 83, Fg St Denis.

Confetti
Manufactured
by
J & E Bella,
113 Charing Cross Rd
London.
W.C.
imp, Bella & de Malherbe London & Paris

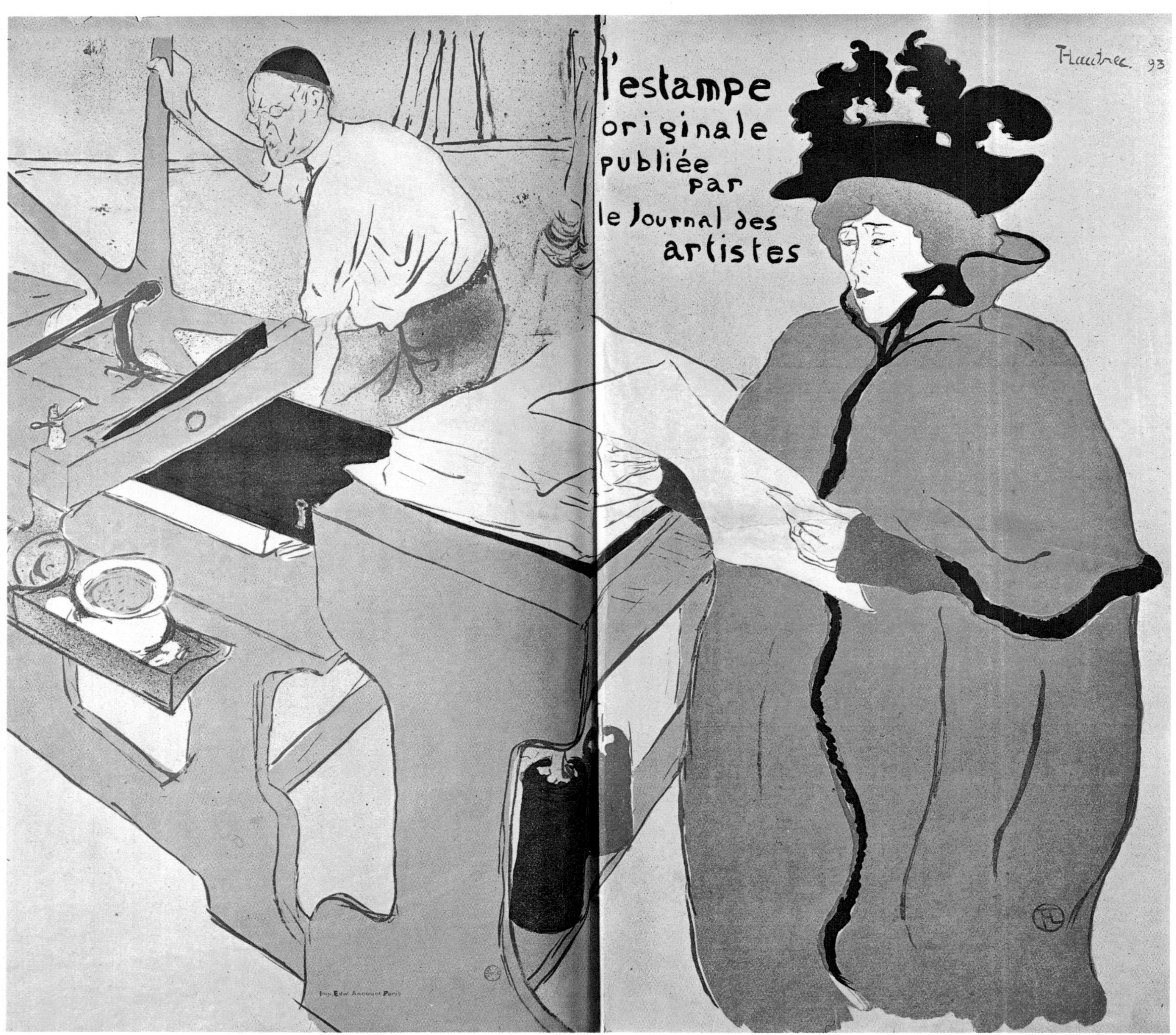
l'estampe
originale
publiée
par
le Journal des
artistes
T-Lautrec 93
Imp. Edw. Ancourt Paris

Caudieux
Imp CHAIX 20 Rue Bergère Paris (Encres Ch. Lorilleux & Cie)
T-Lautrec 93

LIRE
DANS
Le Matin
au Pied
DE
L'ECHAFAUD
MÉMOIRES DE
l'Abbé Faure

aristide
BRUANT
dans son cabaret

16

menu
Potages
St Germain Perles du Japon
Hors d'œuvres
Radis Saucisson crevettes
olives Beurre
Poisson
Filets de Barbue dieppoise
legumes.
Haricots verts maitre d'hotel
petits pois bonne femme
Rots
Dindonneau au cresson
Salade
entremet. Rocher de glace
Desserts assortis
Vins. Bordeaux. Champagne
Café. Cognac
on se mettra
a table à 8 heures

le petit trottin
paroles de
achille Melandri
musique
de
DESIRÉ
DIHAU

Les Vieilles Histoires
Poésies
de Jean Goudezki
mises en musique
par
Désiré Dihau
G. Ondet
éditeur
83. Fg St Denis
à Paris
Prix: 12f
SÉRIE
Tous droits d'exécution, traduction
et reproduction réservés

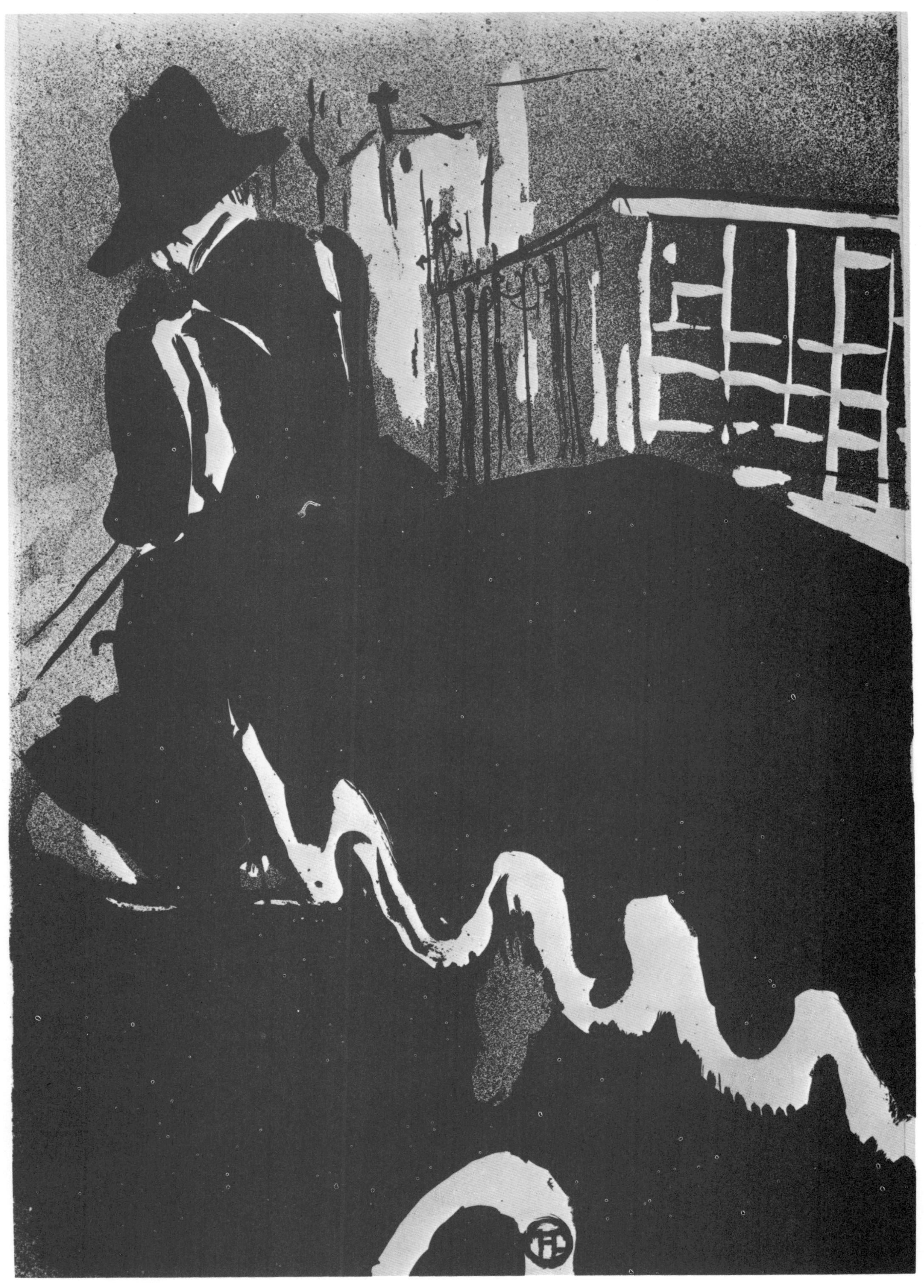

Sagesse

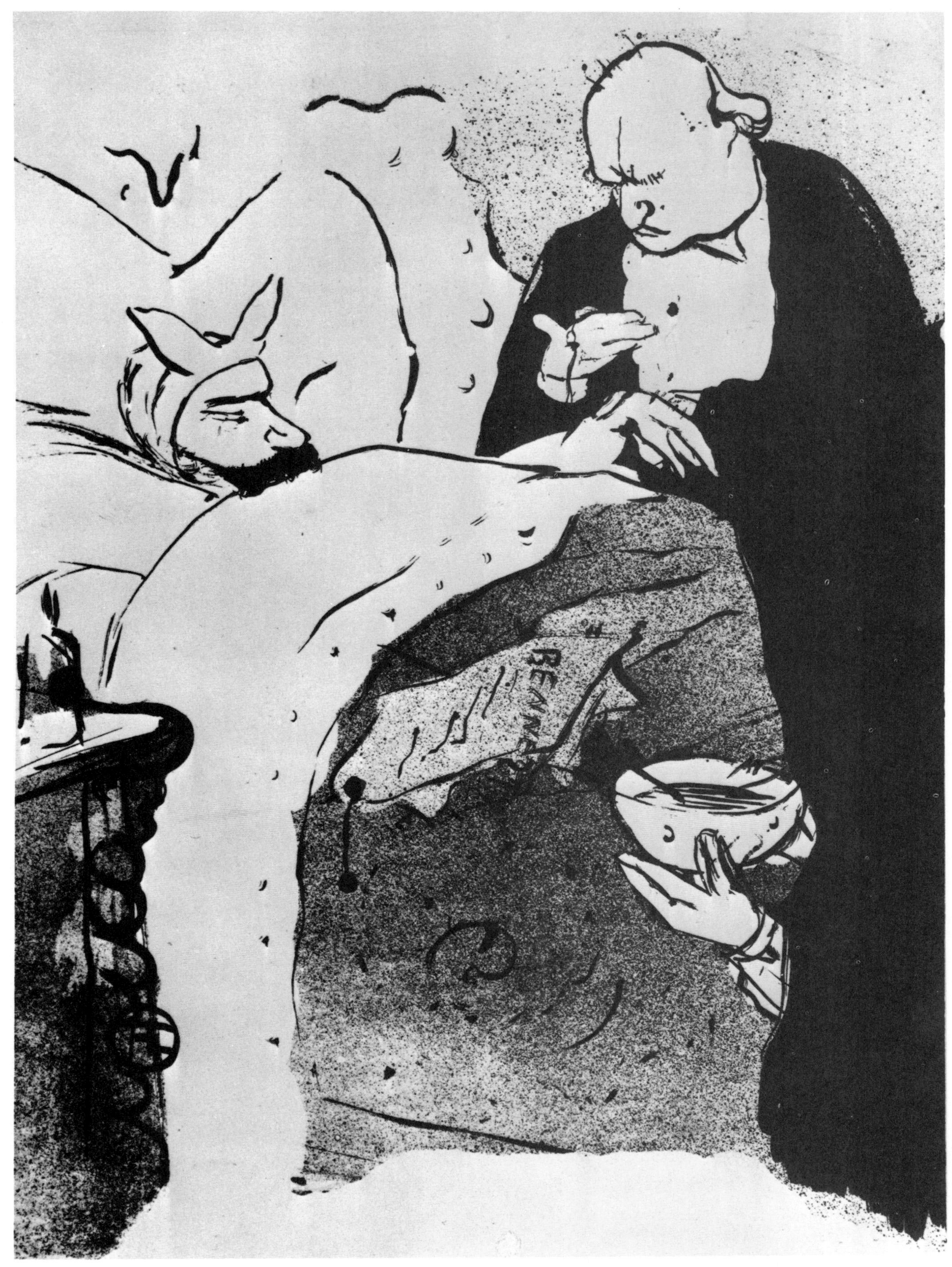

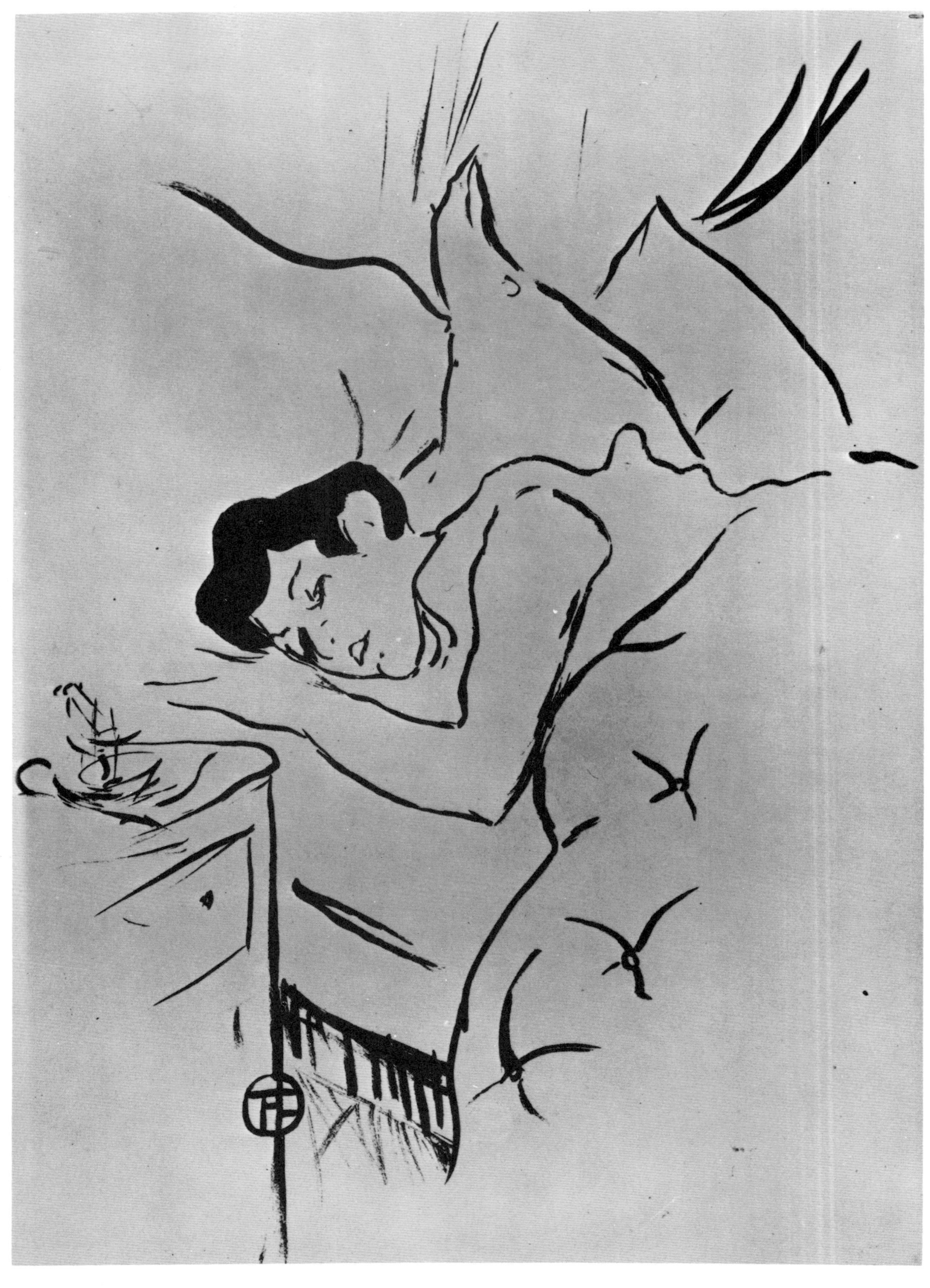

L'Entôleuse
Chanson vécue
Créée par
Mme DE LILDE
le Compositeur CLOËREC-MAUPAS
Renée GILLES
aux Concerts Pacra
Hélène ARNAUD
au Kursaal
Line HERLYS
et
DORIAN
Piano & Cht net: 1.50
Chant seul 0.35
G. ONDET, Editeur
83, Faubg St Denis
PARIS
Tous droits d'exécution de reproduction et de traduction réservés p. t. pays, y compris la Suède & la Norvège
Paroles de
L. GUYOT
Musique de
CLOËREC-MAUPAS

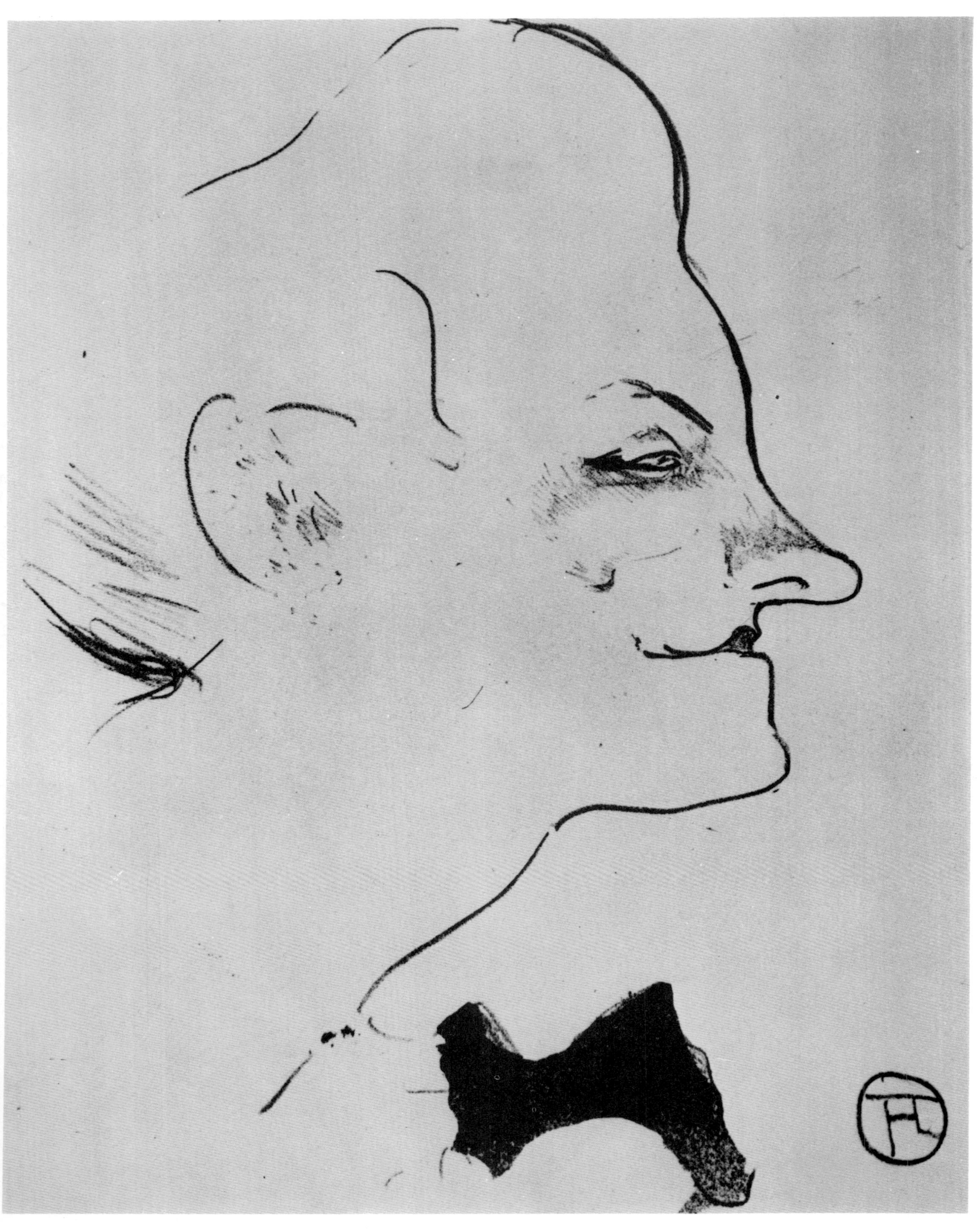

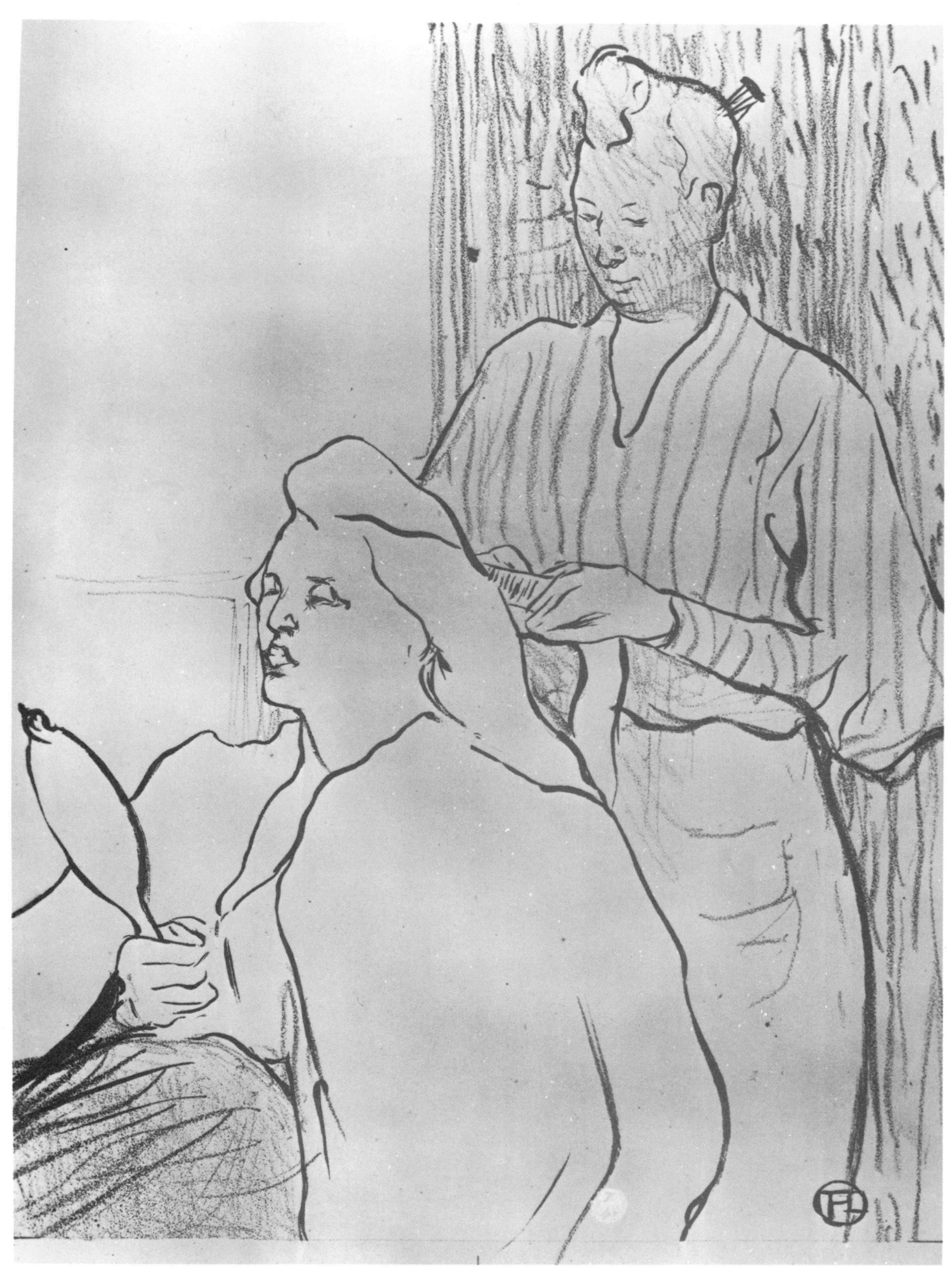

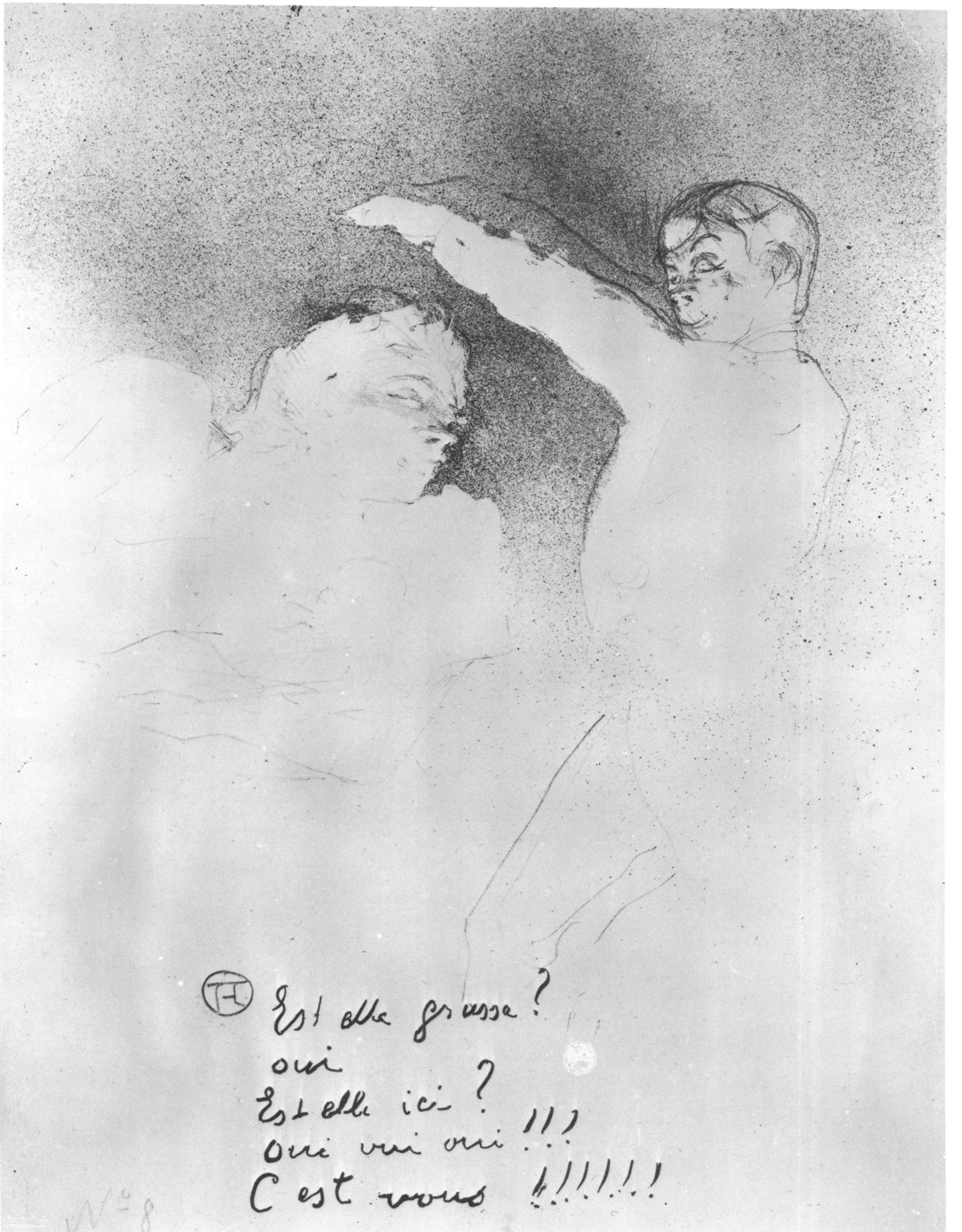
TL
Est elle grasse ?
oui ?
Est elle ici ?
Oui oui oui !!!
C est vous !!!!!!
N° 8

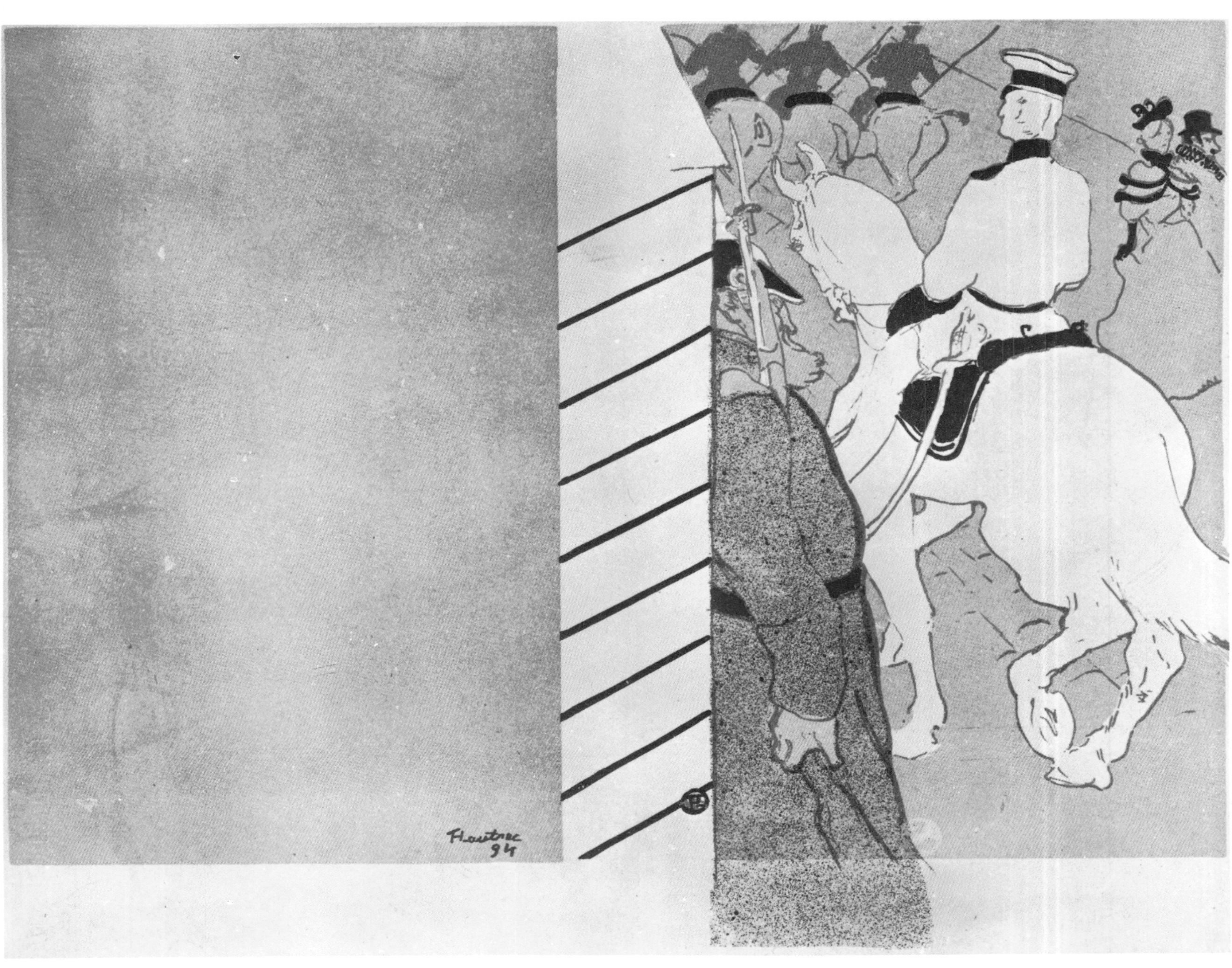

HLautrec
94

Babylone
d'Allemagne
par
Victor JOZE
MŒURS BERLINOISES
CHEZ TOUS LES LIBRAIRES

9, Place Pigalle
P. Sescau
Photograph

NIEDERKORN
l'Artisan Moderne
Objets d'art, meubles, ensembles décoratifs
9. Quai Voltaire
12. rue Bonaparte
39 bis, rue de Châteaudun
25. galerie Vivienne
1. Boulevard des Capucines
20. rue Lafitte
8, rue de la Victoire
7 rue Racine
18, rue Saint-Lazare
19. rue Caumartin

LE THÉATRE LIBRE
5e Spectacle de la Saison
1893-1894
Le Missionnaire
ROMAN THÉATRAL EN CINQ TABLEAUX
Bernard de Juigneux . . . . MM. GÉMIER
Barthélemy de Juigneux . . . LAUDNER
Henri de Juigneux. . . . . ARQUILLIÈRE
Jacques Rébon . . . . . . ÉTIÉVANT
Le Vicomte . . . . PAUL EDMOND
Un Domestique . . . . . . VERSE
Raoule de Juigneux . . . Mmes MARGUERITE ROLLAND
Madame de Marcenay . . . BELLY
La partie de lecture . . . . M. ANTOINE
De la part de M. Marcel LUGUET.

75 74

Créé par YVETTE GUILBERT
LES VIEUX MESSIEURS
MONOLOGUE
PAR
Maurice DONNAY
Prix 1 fr.
SOCIÉTÉ NOUVELLE D'ÉDITIONS MUSICALES (Ancien fonds PAUL DUPONT)

CRÉÉ
par
YVETTE GUILBERT
ADOLPHE
OU
LE JEUNE HOMME TRISTE
PAR
MAURICE DONNAY
Chant et Piano
Pr. 3 fr.
La même, sans Accomp.t
(f.t in 8.o) Pr. 1 fr.
PAUL DUPONT
EDITEUR
4, Rue du Bouloi

26 Avril
94

Yvette
Guilbert
texte
de Gustave Geffroy
orné par
H. de Toulouse Lautrec

·uilbert

on entend qu'elle chante bien, et

: elle prononce, elle articule, elle

vers le jardin des Champs-Élysées,

vapeur d'alcool, la buée des haleines.

par le gosier, par les dents, par la

ansparente, à la fois ferme et frêle

c'est son flair de chanteuse, son air

e dite fin-de-siècle, — l'odieux mot

qu'il faut bien se résigner à écrire.

ne statue gaie et macabre, en chair,

ntendre une voix ennuyée et mor-

rement. La bouche est ironique, le

ace blanche apparaît tout à coup

, elle en a sans doute, mais qui sont

Et puis, elle a sa personne, qu'elle

ntorsions, mais qui n'en reste pas moins une personne ondulante et

elle jaillit des coulisses d'un pas délibéré, et qui se brise et s'évapore

n salut.

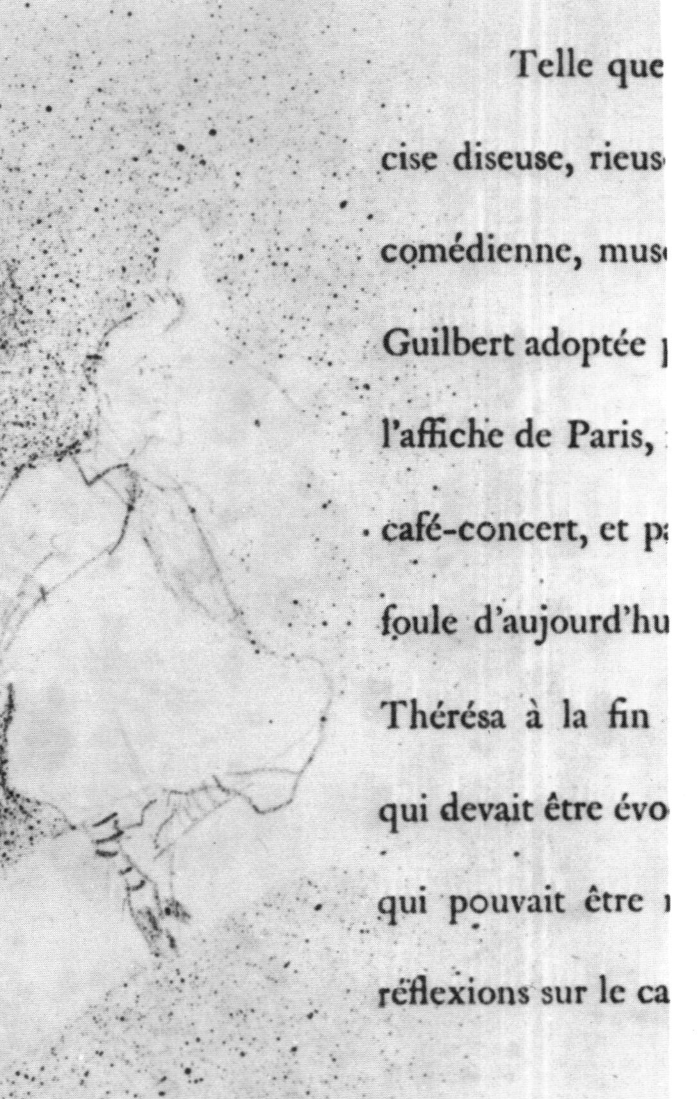

Telle que

cise diseuse, rieus

comédienne, mus

Guilbert adoptée

l'affiche de Paris,

café-concert, et p

foule d'aujourd'hu

Thérésa à la fin

qui devait être évo

qui pouvait être

réflexions sur le ca

Yvette Gu

cert de l'originalité, de la voix, de l'ironie, mais le café-c talents, sans poésie, sans musique, sans rien. Il vivrait ave chanson. Le flamboiement du gaz à la porte, ou la na affiches grimaçantes, des noms en vedette, des visages femmes. A l'intérieur, l'odeur de la bière et du tabac, des rangs gai, un rideau qui se lève, quelqu'un qui apparaît et qui chante pas davantage pour que la foule vienne, compacte et bruyante, au

Quel attrait mystérieux l'attire donc ? Quelle odeur lui indique

Entrez avec elle.

Quoi que l'on chante, et chanté par n'importe qui, si les couplet de la scatologie, la joie sera unanime, vous assisterez au rire brutal, à la pâ

C'est affreux, blessant, et vous,
votre siège, fuirez ce lieu empesté, décla
respirer cette atmosphère, entendre ces c

Il est certain que la répulsion pe
un effroi, un dégoût, une sorte de courba
Et même, il se peut concevoir un senti
rejette néanmoins ceux qui auraient t
acceptés, musiquettes convenues, plates
en trouver dans les théâtres les mieux
femmes rient derrière l'éventail et les hon
l'intellectualité du plaisir admis n'est pas
que la déclaration contre le café-concert,
peut se trouver aussi, chez un grand no
somptions.

Les faits, c'est que le public des ca
jours, et finit par résumer assez bien les di
saison de l'année, de Juillet à Septembre,
placé. C'est l'époque des concerts en plein
installée, cette fois, assez loin des faubourg
affluent, il n'est pas interdit de croire que n
de distraction avec l'été. Comme on chante
quinquets, c'est donc l'atmosphère matérielle qui était, pour beau

La vérité, c'est qu'il n'y a pas, dans une grande ville telle
plutôt, la grande différence crée une infime minorité et une immense maj

choisissent
lecture à
gination.
Po
de chez eu
lumière, le
à eux, de l
En
du café-co
lente santé
du café-co
On
fond remue
souvent é
Ma
cochonneri
donner leu
Co
Qu
les porter a
vous réfléc
poursuit le misérable homme, la pauvre unité so
le nécessaire, sur la paie de la semaine, sur les appointem

e inspection de l'affiche.
ite, il est bien temps de
ies places du parterre au
prises par ceux qui ont pu
s. Il reste les étages supé-
:. Et encore ne faut-il pas

une peine, une humiliation
et pour entendre, ce n'est
ics, ou sept francs, et plus,
it mieux entrer tout de go,
devant un verre, sortir son

t-quatorze, et il va y avoir
ie existe. Depuis ce temps-
retentissants orateurs de la
l'ordre du jour de l'éduca-
rits la nécessité de faire et
ouveau. Mais en pratique,
nt montrés plus timides.
ersistants, des plus tenaces,
l'utilité et la justice ? Seuls
proclament le mal fondé de ce budget d'instruction. Ils diraient volontiers, et ils disent,
faut la religion. Eux peuvent se passer de l'une et de l'autre, et s'en passent, à l'aide de
is de ce monde. Aussi ont-ils inventé les Ecoles fondées sur l'esprit de caste, celles qui

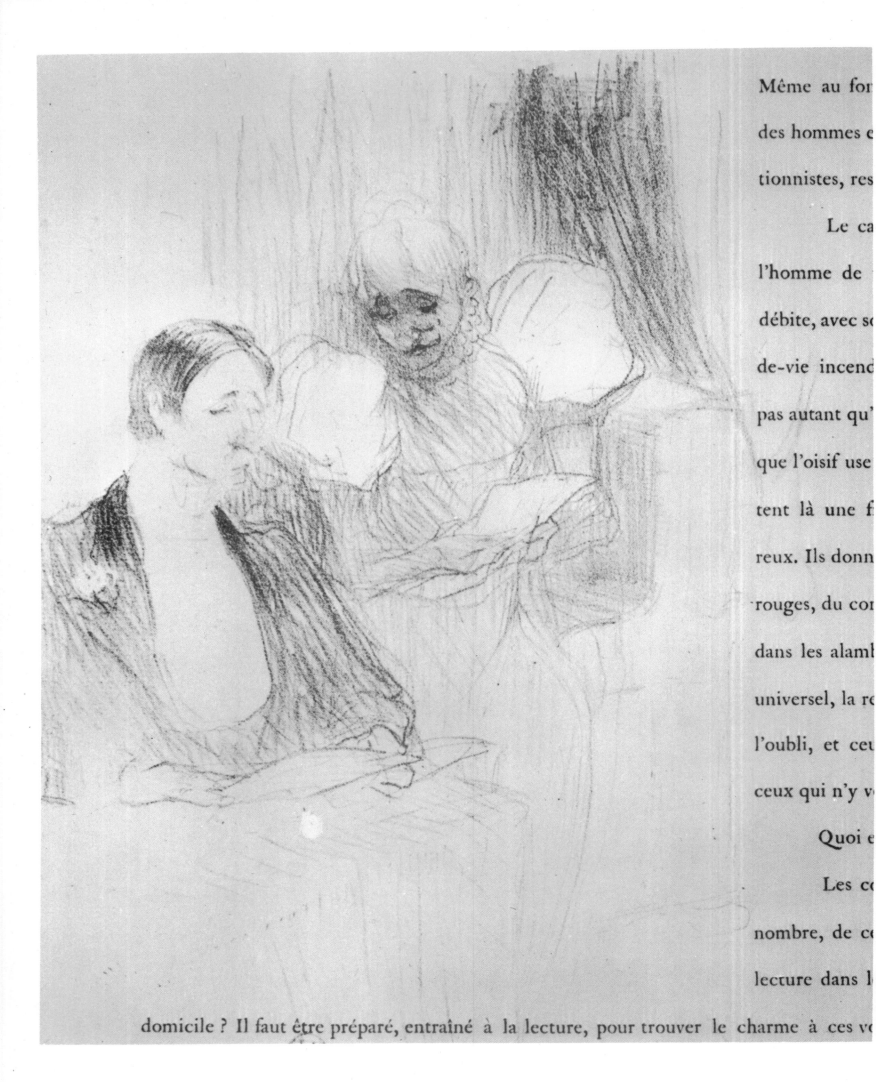

Même au for

des hommes e

tionnistes, res

Le ca

l'homme de

débite, avec so

de-vie incend

pas autant qu'

que l'oisif use

tent là une f

reux. Ils donn

rouges, du con

dans les alamb

universel, la r

l'oubli, et ceu

ceux qui n'y v

Quoi e

Les c

nombre, de c

lecture dans l

domicile ? Il faut être préparé, entraîné à la lecture, pour trouver le charme à ces vo

ioches, l'heure du

que promenade au

en somme. On les

rd du trottoir, ou

théâtre suburbain,

foule, ce que veut

foule bureaucrate

nis. Elle veut de la

, la gaîté du petit

e défaite, les mains

llant, et l'entendre

ctions humaines

ême de jeter une
ons de la vie. Ils
l'une des tradi-

ercher toutes les
pays flottante au-
a Bourgogne au
difficile, à ceux
apeur de terroir.
Et son réalisme
érébralité alerte,
as été fait un élé-

isme de la race
l'être. La natio-
bon docteur qui
njoint d'accepter

qui se payent de
recueilli de la haute philosophie du vaste esprit, de son

cela du nom que vous voudrez,
ésolez-vous de sa niaiserie et de
alité inférieure est du fait de ceux
ceux qui l'écoutent. C'est la vile
la voix du ténor lorsqu'il rou-
ux promenades par les champs, à
complices des chutes, des aban-
is. C'est la servitude que prêche
se ruer aux champs de bataille,
qu'il donne à adorer le cheval
bre.

malheureux à l'écoute, bouche
de vil, c'est par des mots géné-
yance à quelque motif vague et
'elle est réaliste, cette foule est
de l'humanité, et elle n'a pas
t ceux qui prononcent ces mots
galvaudent, qui les érigent en
ais lieux. Ecrivains sadiques ou
e tribune parlementaire ou de
ice exploiteuse de la crédulité.
le et profond sentiment, la poésie vitale, et la patrie, annonciatrice d'humanité, le lien

Aussi, dit-on, ce

trouvé bon. Chaque fois c

Quoi donc?

Le reproche, c'es

de suite le feu d'artifice

Drapeau pour aller au Pl

luxure, à l'ivresse.

Plaisant et funèb

s'aperçoivent-ils pas du si

bas qui les choque, non c

ment fatal. La corruption

dation, se répand partout,

atteintes. Pendant longter

qu'ils la garderaient pour

verait une compensation s

meuses. De même que l'o

sons identiques le plaisi

oublient vraiment par tro

eux si délicieux. Ils se nourrissent d'autres fest

qui les regardaient manger d'un air si heure

dirigeants n'ont pas dirigé, ils ont dépravé. L'histoire

sous Louis XV. On y a mis le fer sous Louis XVI, mais la contagion

Ils en donnent un, i
geignent que le peuple ait p
qui serait étonnant. Si l'esprit
dans une partie de la populat
cela tout ce qu'il fallait. Tout
l'on appelle la société. Des h
lette autant que les femmes, v
leur ventre comme un dieu.
trouperaient-ils pas au défil
restaurants chics, et ne finirai
y a des dessous aux déclaratio
aperçus, une débauche à pein
siaque d'une quinzaine ou d'
mariage d'argent. Et pourquo
gagner leur vie et qui ne co
deux, les nourritures insuffisa
de naturel, rien que du falsifi
ne s'aviseraient-ils pas d'être
hommes, c'est-à-dire envieux
curieux de ce qui s'affiche a
s'en iraient-ils pas à la dérive
respectable vieillesse qui défilent devant eux, ramollies et joyeus

Ne cherchez pas ailleurs que dans l'homme semblable à l'homme les raisons du déverg
cynisme qui vous effraie. Ceux qui ne peuvent pas avoir la réalité des choses veulent au moins en a
Ils s'en vont donc là où le fumet cherché affectera leurs narines, ils iront se récréer de la niaiser

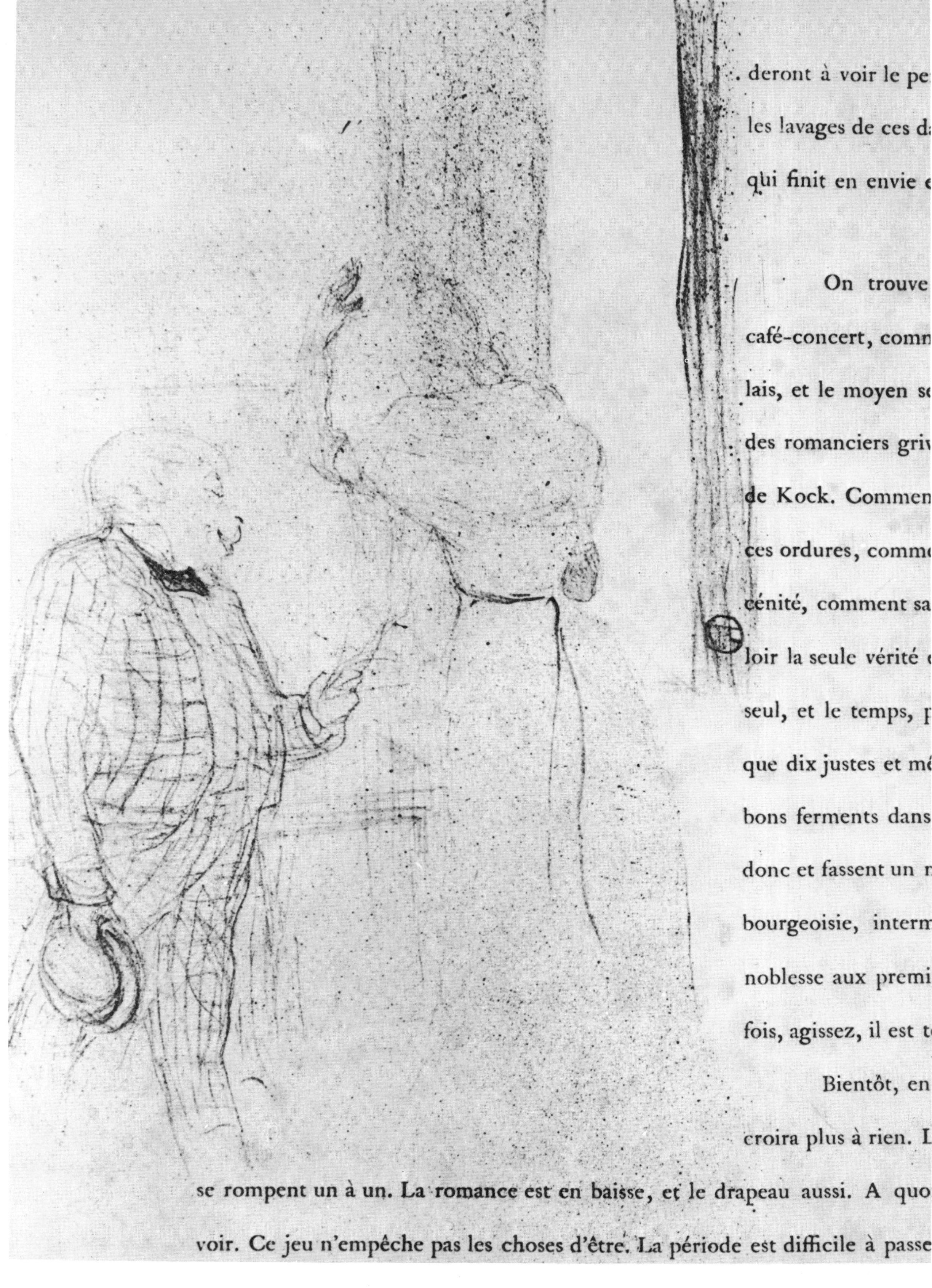

deront à voir le pe

les lavages de ces d

qui finit en envie e

On trouve

café-concert, comm

lais, et le moyen s

des romanciers gri

de Kock. Commen

ces ordures, comm

cénité, comment sa

loir la seule vérité

seul, et le temps, p

que dix justes et m

bons ferments dans

donc et fassent un

bourgeoisie, interm

noblesse aux premi

fois, agissez, il est t

Bientôt, en

croira plus à rien. L

se rompent un à un. La romance est en baisse, et le drapeau aussi. A quo

voir. Ce jeu n'empêche pas les choses d'être. La période est difficile à passe

NIB

2e Saison 1894-95
4me soirée
Le Chariot de Terre Cuite
Cinq actes de M. Victor BARRUCAND
d'après la Mric'Chakatika
Conférence de M. Téodor de WYZEWA
Décors du 5e acte de M. H. de Toulouse-Lautrec
— 2e — MM. André et Veltat
Exécutés par M. L. de la Quintinie
Costumes de "L'Œuvre"
PERSONNAGES
Vasantasenâ . . . . Mlle Meuris
Madanikâ . . . Mlle Suzanne Desprès
Radanikâ . . . . . Mme Suzanne Gay
Une esclave . . Mlle Georgette Loyer
Tchâroudatta . . . . MM. Ripert
Samsthanaka . . . . Marcel Deslouis
Çarvilaka . . . . Dupont
Maitreya . . . . Tressy
Le Vita . . . . Lugné-Poe
Sthâvaraka . . . . R. Lagrange
Le Çramana . . . . Vague
Aryaka . . . . Kabis
Gohâ . . . . Jablin
Ahintâ . . . . Dujeu
Un brâhmane . . . . . Henry Sérusier
Un artisan . . . . Engel-Ley
Un marchand . . . . Chevillot
Rohasena . . . . X.
Un crieur . . . . Philipon
Brahmanes, guerriers, marchands, artisans, yoghis, çramanas, musiciens, psylles, mendiants, soldats, citadins, policiers, bandhoulas, courtisanes et danseuses
Autrefois dans l'Inde.
मृच्छकटिका

Victor Barrucand
Le Chariot de
Terre cuite
d'après la
मृच्छकटिका
PARIS
bert Savine . Editeur
Rue des Pyramides

Mars 1895
"L'Estampe originale"
Album de clôture
Albert Besnard
Eugène Carrière
Alexandre Charpentier
Walter Crane
Gandara
Constantin Meunier
Camille Pissarro
Puvis de Chavannes
H de Toulouse-Lautrec
Odilon Redon
Renoir
Pierre Roche
Félicien Rops
Willette

Imp. ANCOURT, Paris
TOUTES CES DAMES AU THÉATI
Miam, Miam, Miam....

La revue
blanche
bi-mensuelle
le nº 60 cent.
12 francs par An
1 rue Laffitte
Paris
Charpentier et Fasquelle, éditeurs
11, rue de Grenelle

May Belfort
Edw. Ancourt Paris

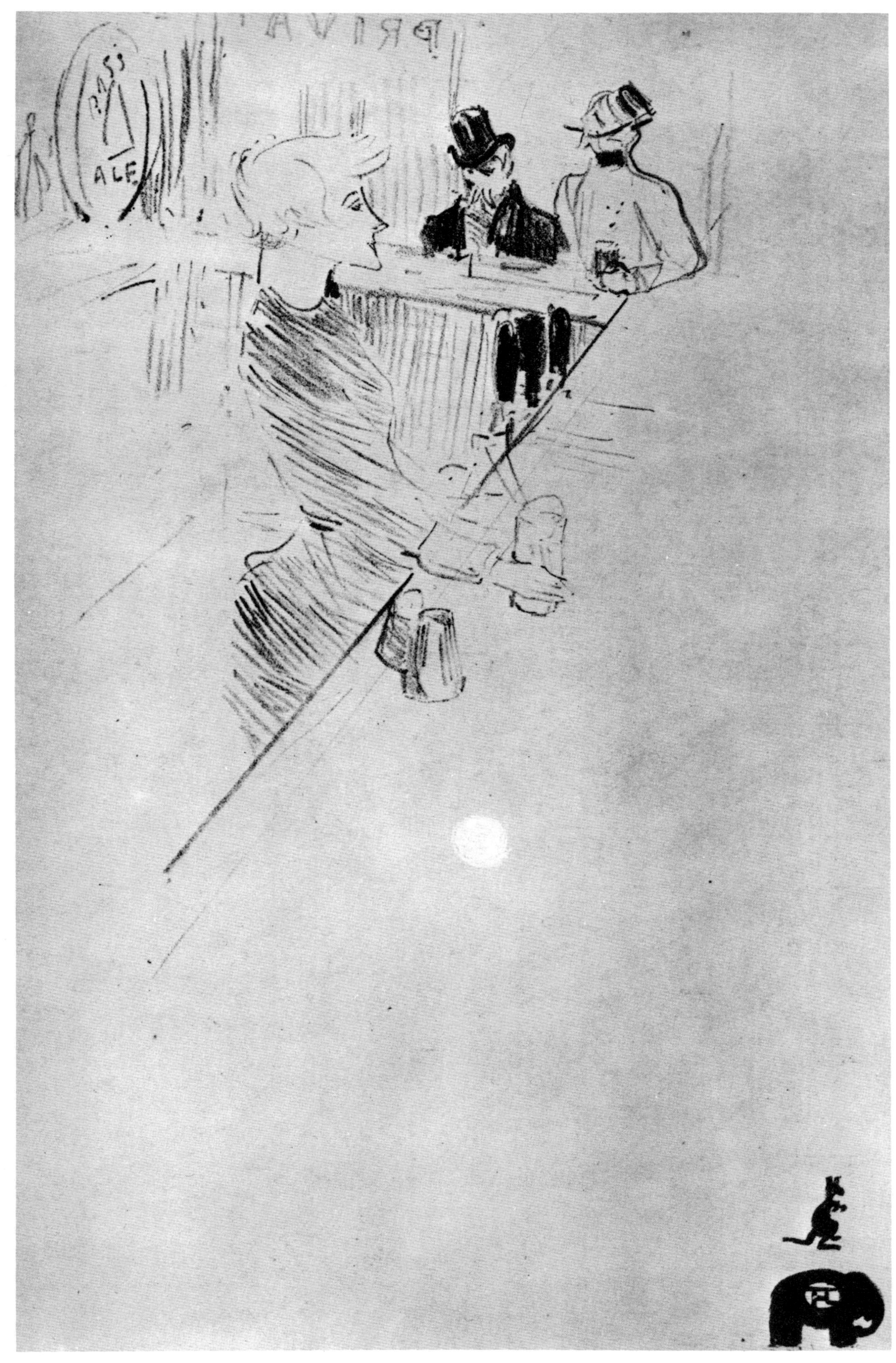
ALE

16 Mars 1895

53, Rue Rodier

MENU

La Bouillabaisse

Hors d'œuvre

Salmis de Perdrix bojé tzaria Krani

L'Agnelet roti

Le Sarigue en Liberty

Salads

Foies gras de l'oïe Fuller

Vegetables

Pièce humide

Cheese and Fruits

Ti Noir

Pivre Lilas Frotteurs

&

Champagne Charlie

Prix : 2 francs
Paul Ollendorff, éditeur
28bis Rue de Richelieu
Paris
1895
TRISTAN BERNARD
Les Pieds nickelés
1 acte

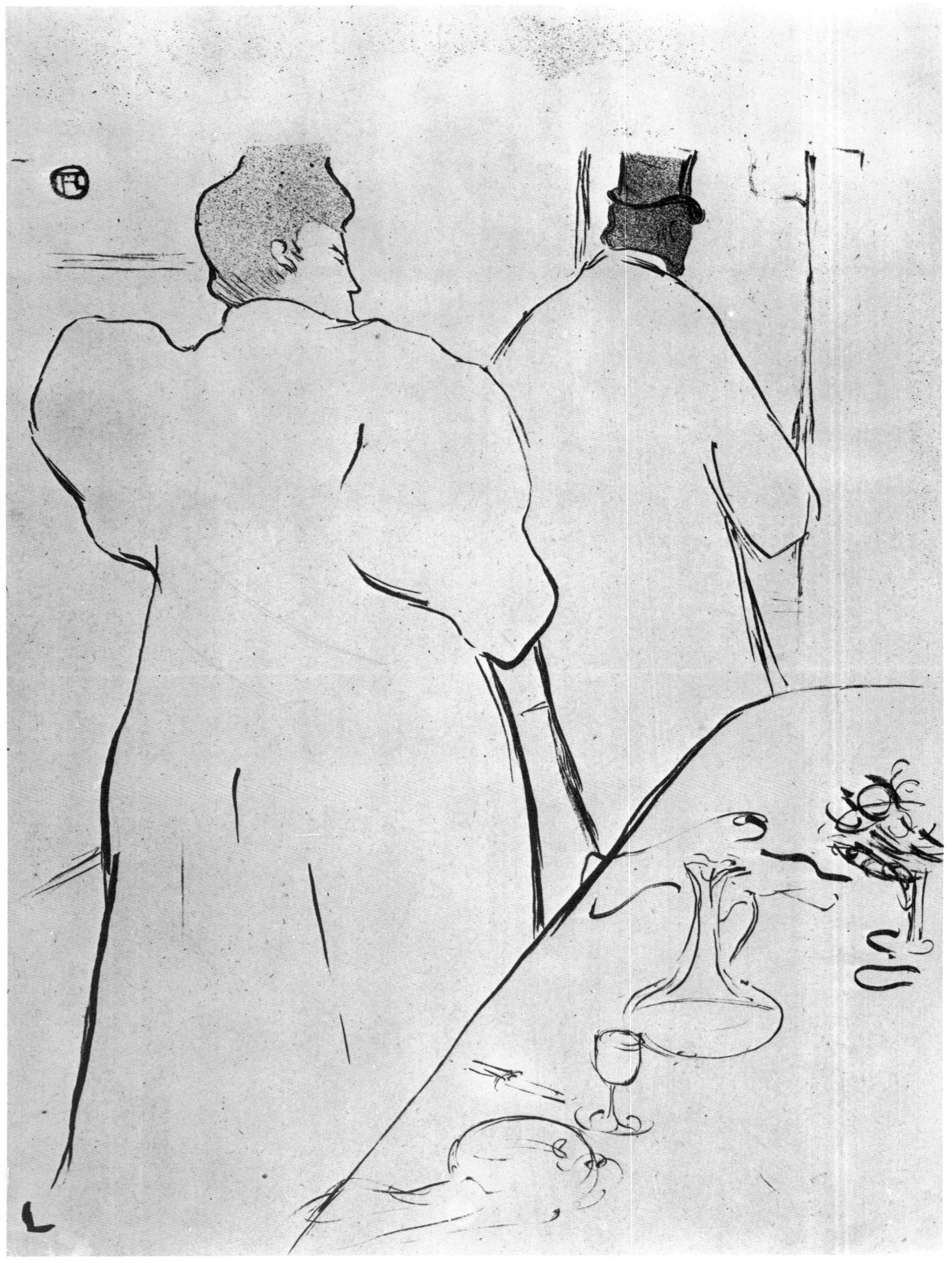

May Mi
ton

A Monsieur Germain DELEBECQUE
Les
HIRONDELLES DE MER
Chanson
Paroles de
Jean RICHEPIN
Musique de
Désiré DIHAU
Piano: net 1f 75
Pt Format: net 0f 30
C. JOUBERT Editeur, 25, Rue d'Hauteville.
Paris
Belgique
KATTO à Bruxelles
Allemagne, Autriche-Hongrie.
BREITKOPF et HÄRTEL à Leipzig.
Tous droits de Traduction, de Reproduction et de Représentation réservés pour tous pays.

A Madame BERTRAND
BALLADE DE NOËL
Chantée par
Francis MARTY
Chantée par LASSALLE de l'Opéra
Piano: 1f35 net
Pt Format: 0.30 net
Poésie de
Jean RICHEPIN
Musique de
Désiré DIHAU
C. JOUBERT Editeur, 25, Rue d'Hauteville
Paris
Imp. Crevel frès Paris
Belgique.
KATTO à Bruxelles
Allemagne, Autriche-Hongrie.
BREITKOPF et HARTEL à Leipzig.
Tous droits de Traduction, de Reproduction et de Représentation réservés pour tous pays.

la Valse des Lapins

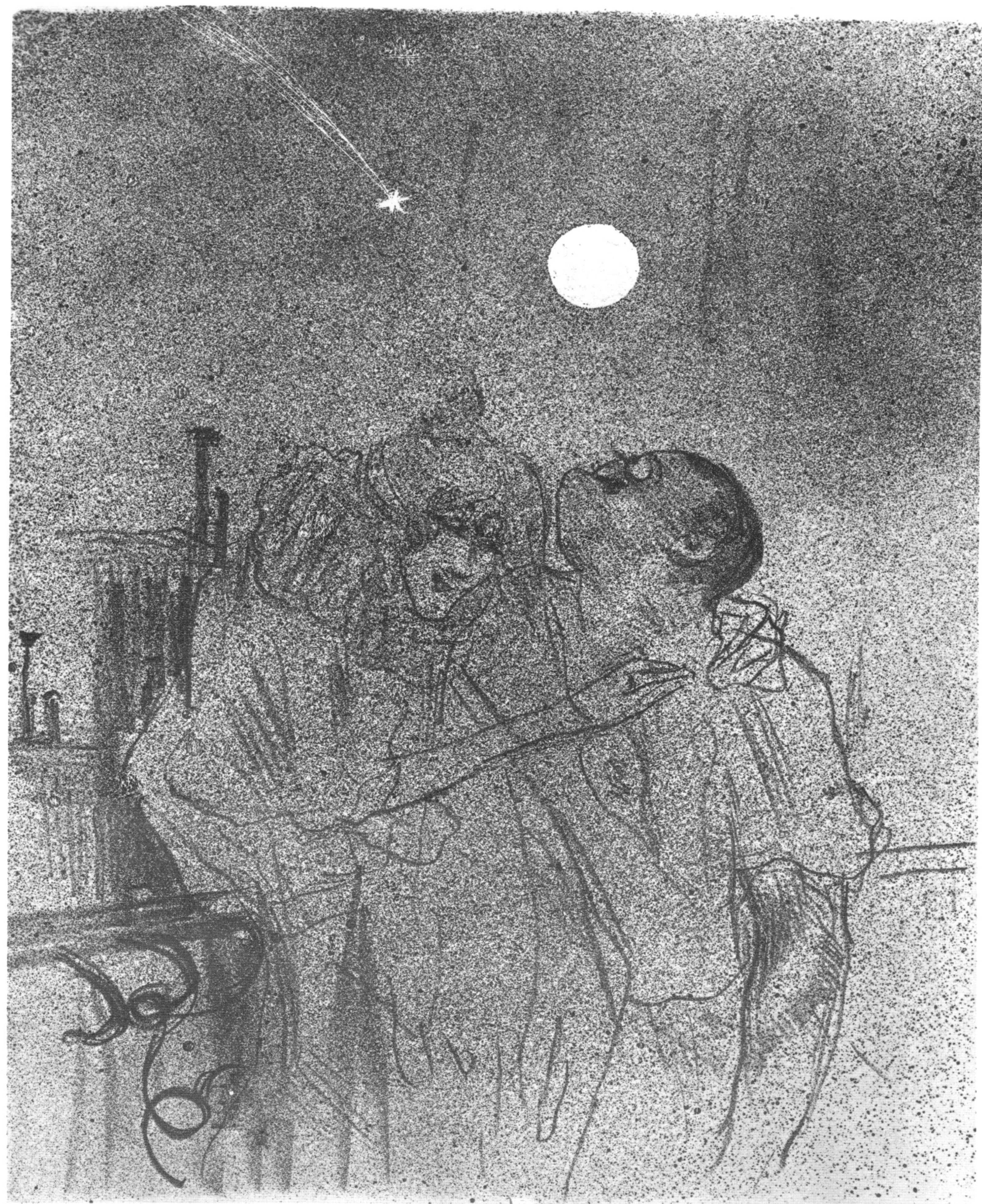

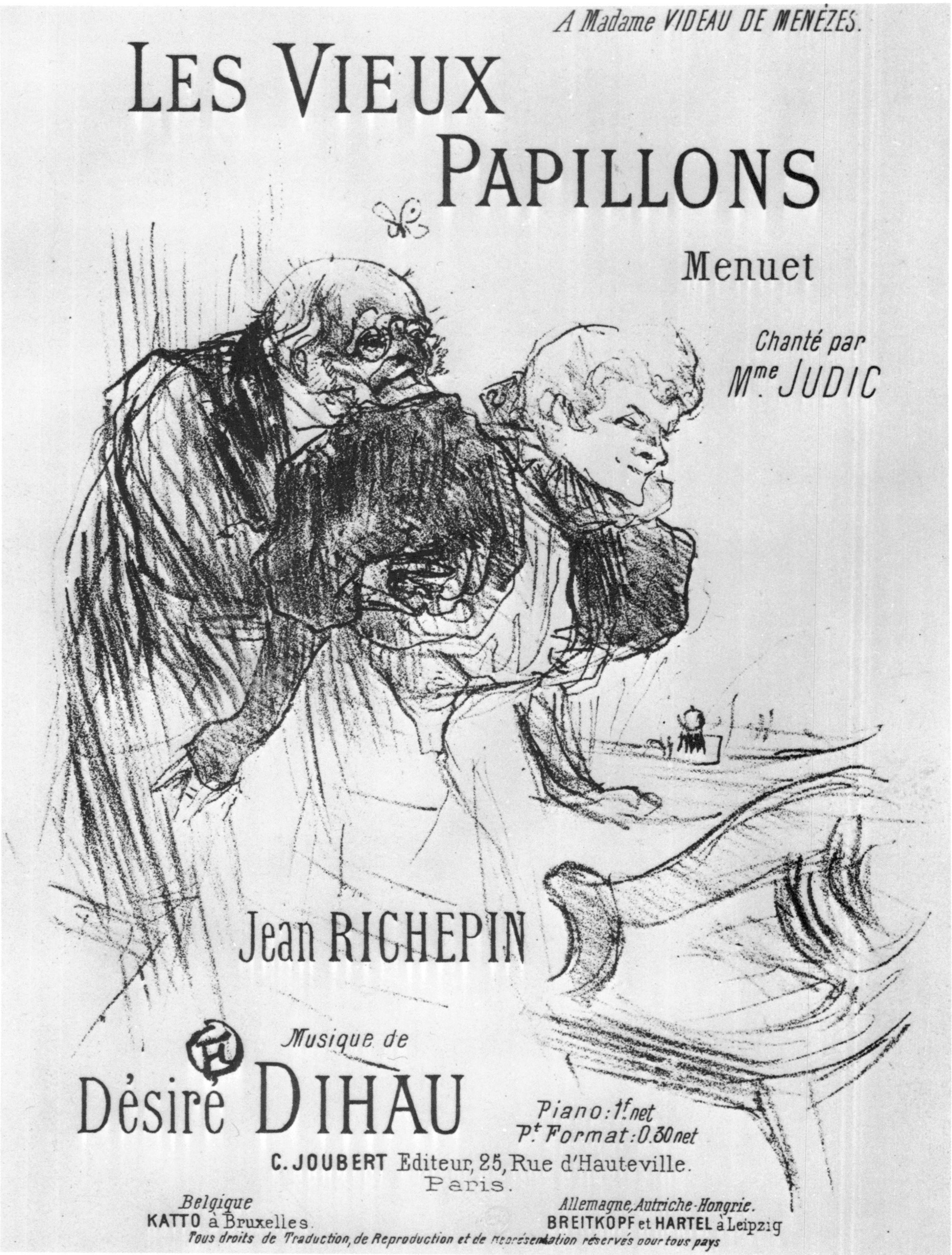

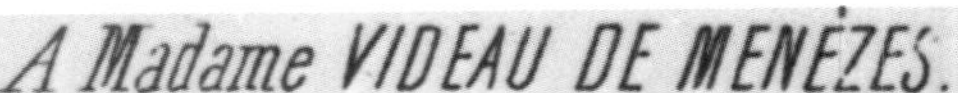

A Madame VIDEAU DE MENÉZES.
LES VIEUX PAPILLONS
Menuet
Chanté par
Mme JUDIC
Jean RICHEPIN
Musique de
Désiré DIHAU
Piano: 1f. net
Pt. Format: 0.30 net
C. JOUBERT Editeur, 25, Rue d'Hauteville.
Paris.
Belgique
KATTO à Bruxelles.
Allemagne, Autriche-Hongrie.
BREITKOPF et HARTEL à Leipzig
Tous droits de Traduction, de Reproduction et de Représentation réservés pour tous pays

A VILLE
Le Fou
Chanson
Piano: 1f net
Pt Format: 0.30 net
Paroles de
Jean RICHEPIN
Musique de
Désiré DIHAU
C. JOUBERT Editeur, 25, Rue d'Hauteville
Paris
Belgique.
KATTO à Bruxelles
Allemagne, Autriche-Hongrie.
BREITKOPF et HÄRTEL à Leipzig.
Tous droits de Traduction, de Reproduction et de Représentation réservés pour tous pays.

96
No — 200

96
COMÉDIE-PARISIENNE
Au Bénéfice de Madame Louise FRANCE
PREMIÈRE REPRÉSENTATION
DE
LA LÉPREUSE
Tragédie Légendaire en 3 Actes
DE M. HENRY BATAILLE
Distribution :
La Vieille Lili .... MMmes L. FRANCE
Aliette .... BERTHE BADY
Maria Kantck .... R. DE PONTRY
Renée .... F. SAEZINGER
Genovefa .... JULIETTE VARY
Anaïk .... HEDVIGE MORE
Fantik .... B. SERAPHINO
Ervoanik .... MMrs PAUL FRANCK
Matelinn Kantck .... RAYMOND
Le Sénéchal .... DEMEYER
Le Recteur .... St-CHARLES
Un Paysan .... VERSE
Paysans, Paysannes, etc.
L'action se passe en Bretagne au XVe Siècle.

"l'Œuvre"
administration : 23, rue Turgot
TROISIÈME SAISON
QUATRIÈME SPECTACLE
Raphaël
Pièce en trois actes de M. ROMAIN COOLUS
Louisa .... MM^mes Faustine Chartier
Rita .... Suzanne Auclair
Daniel .... MM. F. Gémier
Mignard .... Reigers
Raphaël .... Nerey
Jonathan .... Lajeunesse
Les Meubles et Objets d'Art ont été mis à notre disposition par « l'Art Nouveau »
Salomé
Pièce en un acte d'OSCAR WILDE
Salomé .... MM^mes Lina Munte
Hérodias .... Barbieri
Le page d'Hérodias ..... Suzanne Auclair
Une esclave .... Hedwige Moore
Esclaves d'Hérodias : Mmes Fanny Zaessinger, Brothel, Renouard, Moore, Urgèle, Auclair.
Iokanaan .... MM. Max Barbier
Hérode .... Lugné-Poe
Le jeune Syrien .... Nerey
Un juif .... Labruyère
1er soldat .... Lévêque
[illegible] .... Laumonnier
2e soldat .... Griffon
Le Nazaréen ... J. Hemgé
Le Cappadocien Lajeunesse
Nazaréens, Juifs, Romains, etc. : MM. Favrel, Biron, Latchat, Bauffre.
Décor de M. H. SÉRUZIER
Musique de scène de M. René LARDÉ
La REVUE ENCYCLOPÉDIQUE est désormais hebdomadaire et paraît tous les samedis, en fascicules de 20 pages illustrées, du prix de 50 centimes.
La REVUE ENCYCLOPÉDIQUE est la seule revue qui consigne toutes les manifestations importantes de l'esprit moderne, la seule qui ait fait jusqu'ici une large place aux tentatives d'art marquées du sceau de la personnalité.
Édition d'amateur
La REVUE ENCYCLOPÉDIQUE se publie en tirage spécial exécuté à petit nombre (500 exemplaires) sur papier couché. Cette superbe édition met plus complètement en valeur la beauté des gravures de la Revue, et contient, hors texte, des reproductions de chefs-d'œuvre de l'art ancien et moderne. 26 planches ont été ainsi publiées en 1895. L'année 1896 en comprendra un nombre égal; mais, toujours soucieuse de progrès, la Revue Encyclopédique les choisira de manière à donner à la collection un plus grand intérêt d'art. Parmi ces 26 planches, douze estampes originales, lithographies, eaux-fortes, bois, glyptographies, etc., qui représentent une valeur bien supérieure au prix de l'abonnement, seront signées : Dagnan-Bouveret, Ribot, Fantin-Latour, Jules Chéret, Henri Guérard, Lepère, Maurice Dumont, etc.
Nota. — L'Édition d'amateur ne se vend pas au numéro. Prix de l'abonnement d'un an : France, 50 francs; Étranger, 60 francs.
LIBRAIRIE LAROUSSE, 17

La Chaîne Simpson
L.B. SPOKE
DIRECTEUR POUR LA FRANCE
25, Boulevard Haussmann.
IMPRIMERIE CHAIX,

LA VACHE ENRAGEE

journal mensuel illustré

Paris: 12f par an

fondateur: A. Willette

directeur: A. Roedel

le n°: 1f.

à l'ami Simonet

RUE BERGÈRE, 20 PARIS

administration: 7, rue androuet, Paris.

Troupe de
Mlle ÉGLANTINE
Eglantine
Jane Avril
Cléopatre
Gazelle

THE
AULT & WIBORG CO
MAKERS OF
FINE PRINTING
AND LITHOGRAPHIC
INKS
COPYRIGHTED BY CHAS. H. AULT, CLEVELAND, O.
CINCINNATI-NEW YORK-CHICAGO

ELLES
par

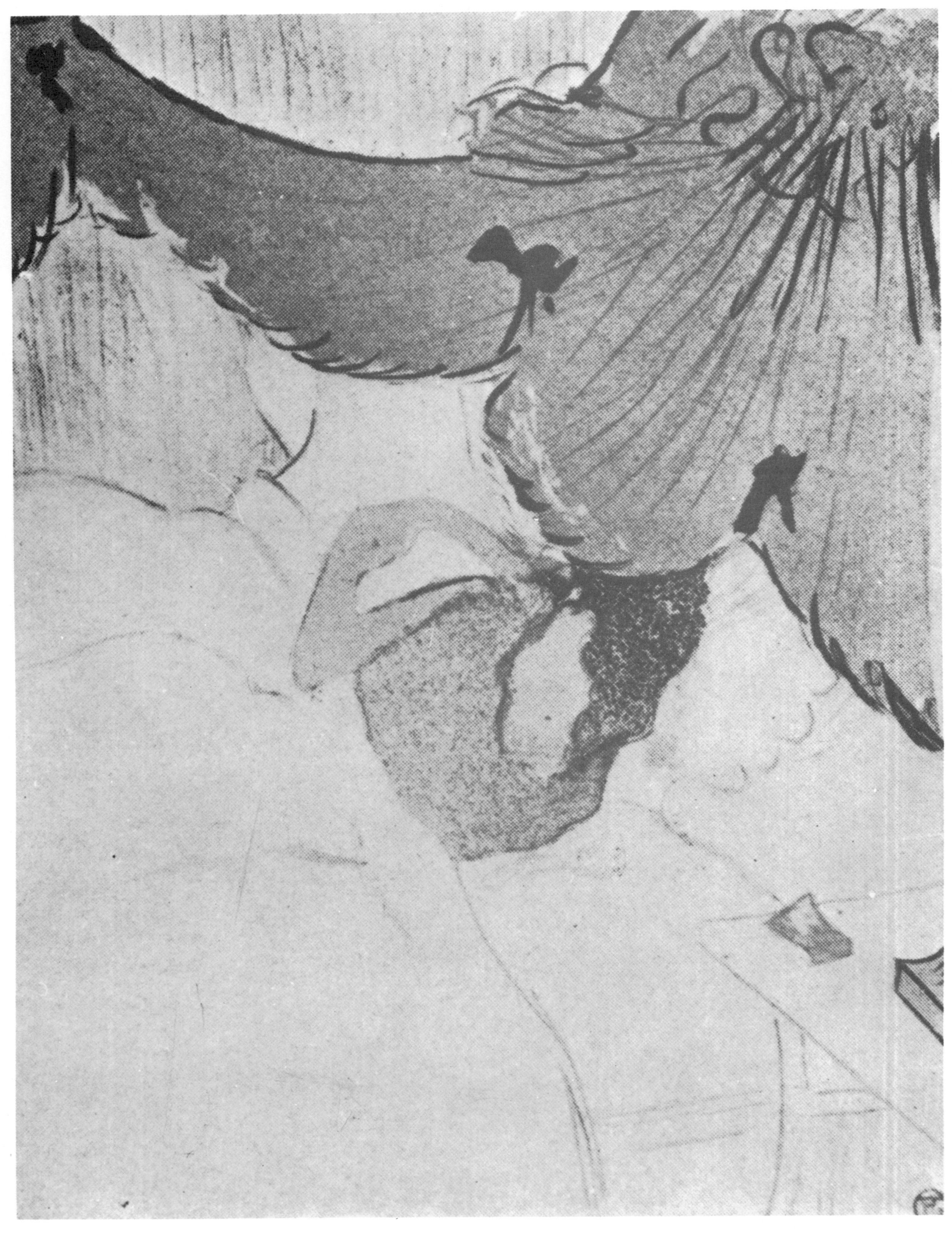

L'Aube
revue
illustrée
26 quai d'Orléans

Dîner des Tarnais

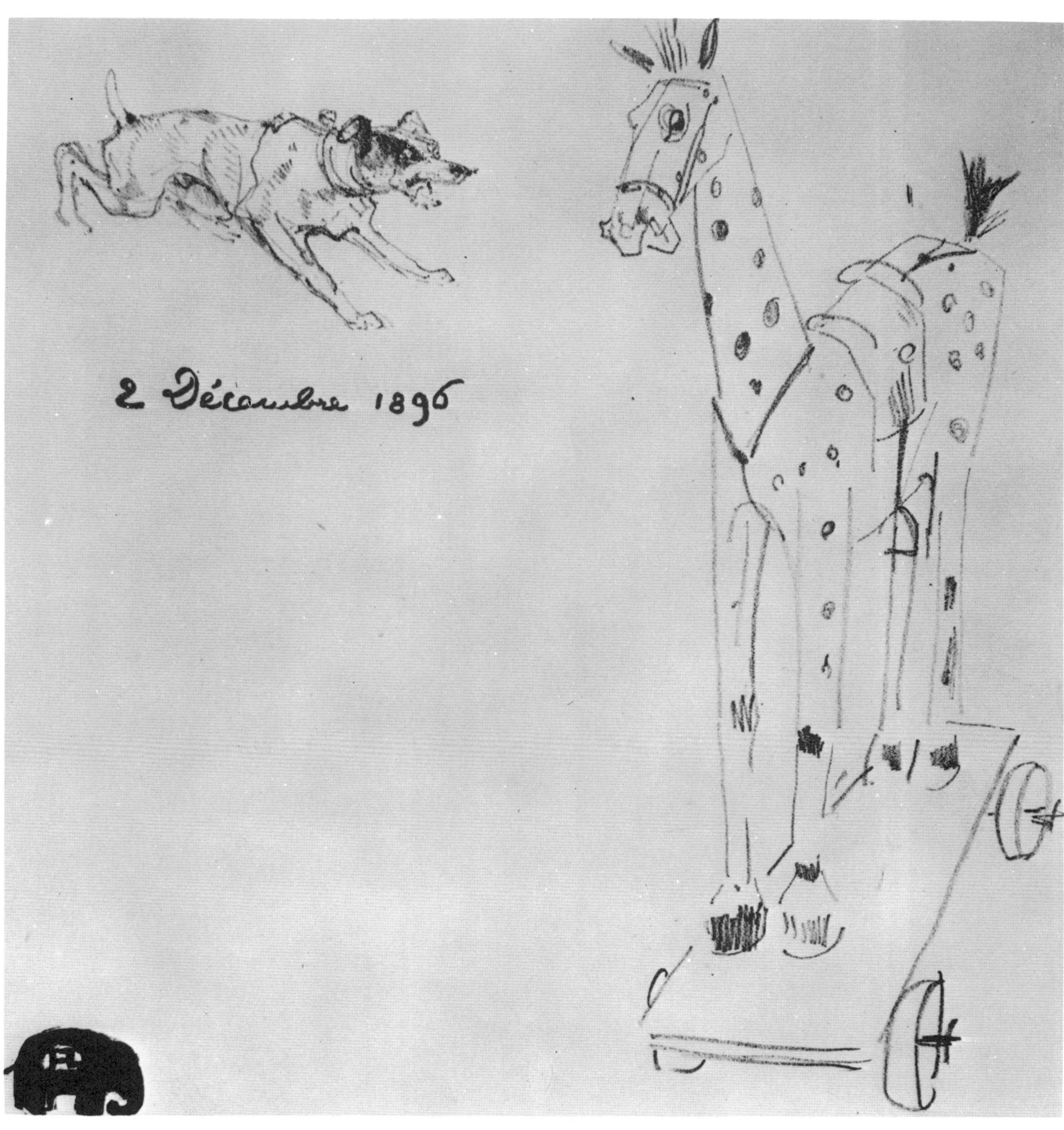
2 Décembre 1896

Dîner du 23 Décembre 18
Huitres de Burnham
Consommé Royal — Potage St-Hubert

a merry christmas
and a happy
new year

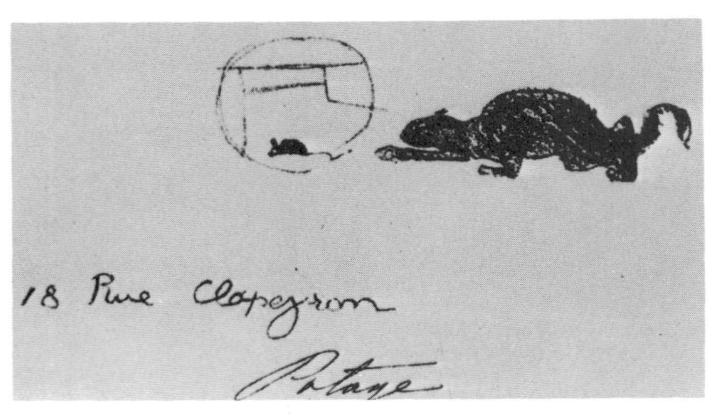

5 avenue Frochot
Henri de Toulouse Lautrec sera très flatté si vous voulez
bien accepter une tasse de lait le samedi 15 Mai
vers 3 heures et demie après midi

Répertoire YVAIN

A mon Père

Les Rois Mages

Légende

Poésie de

L. Delormel et P. Maly

Musique de

Désiré Dihau

Prix 3 fr.

Paris, QUINZARD Cie Editeurs, 24, rue des Capucines

Madrid
1863
Los Desastres
de la Guerra
por Don Francisco Goya

G. Clemenceau
Au pied du Sinai
Au pied
du Sinai
illustré
H. de Toulouse-Lautrec
Editeur

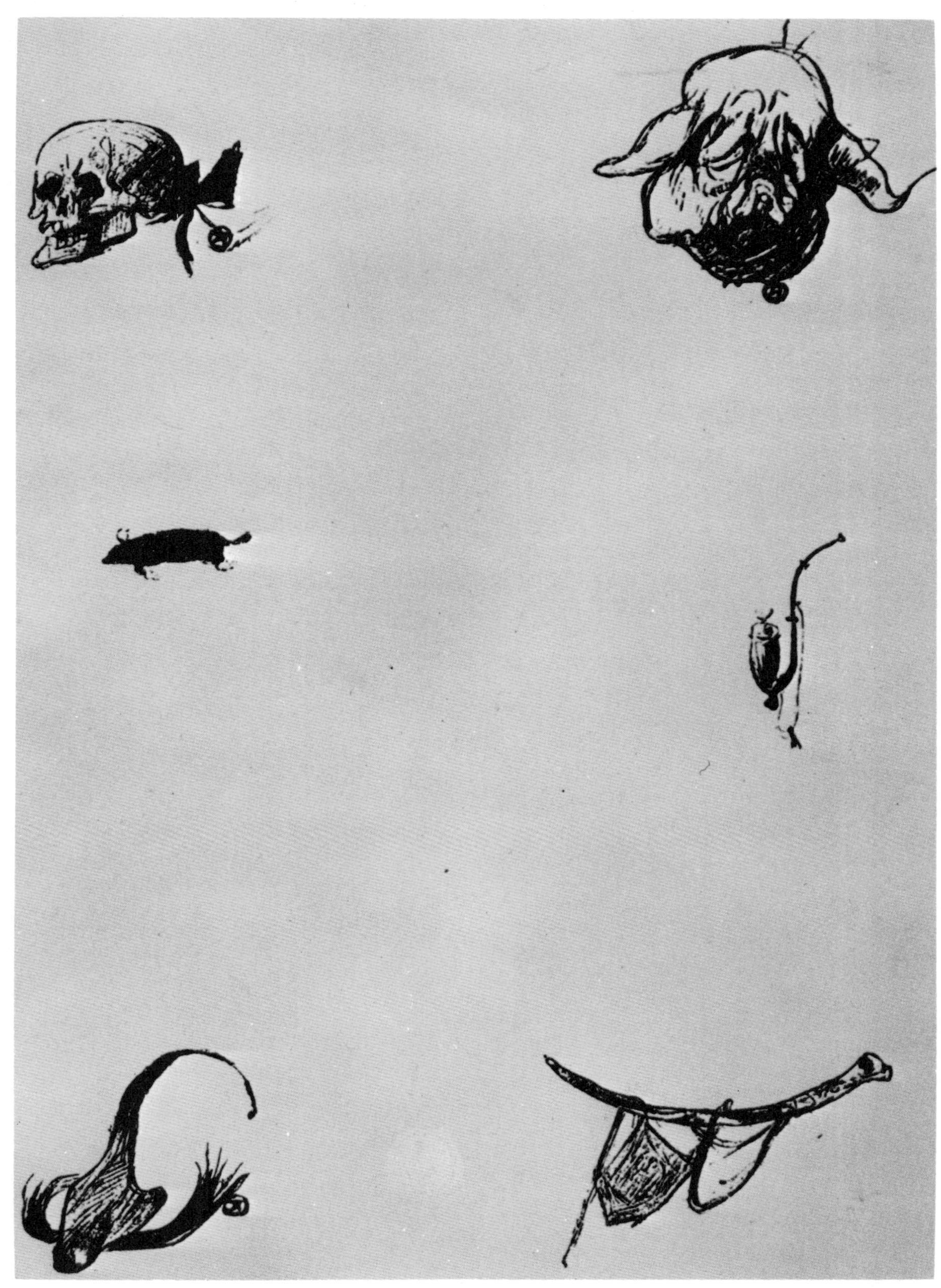

Menu

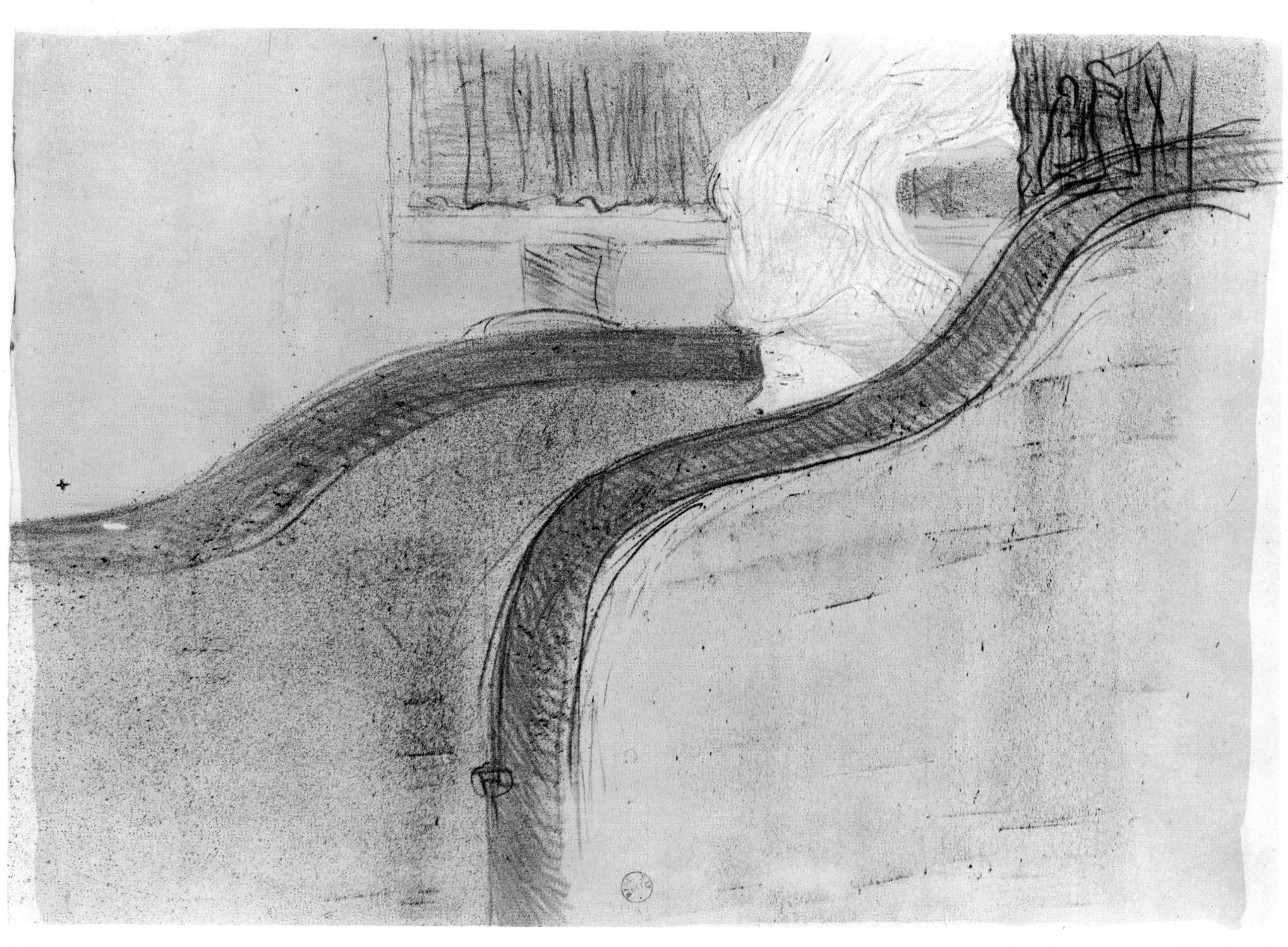

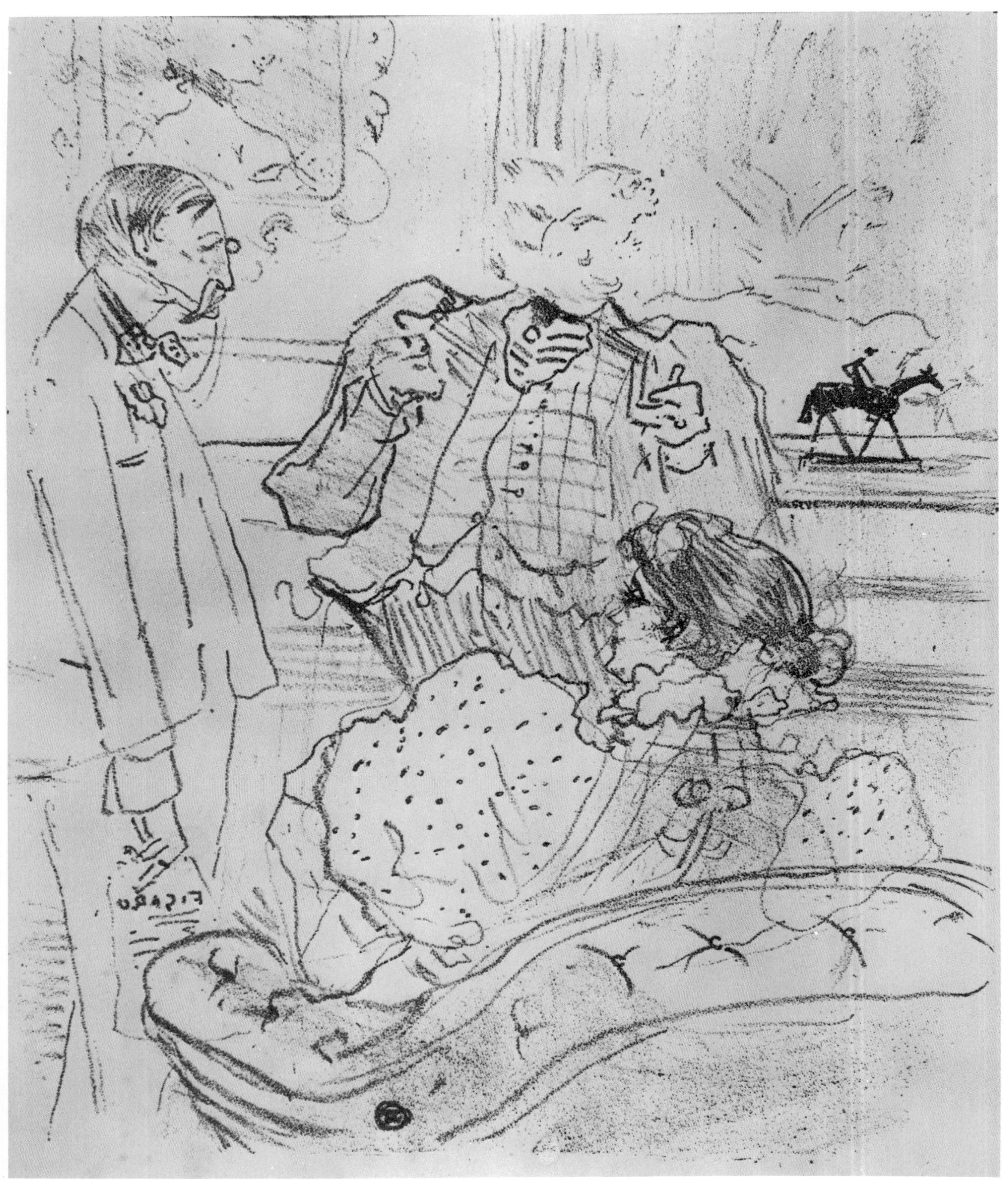
FIGARO

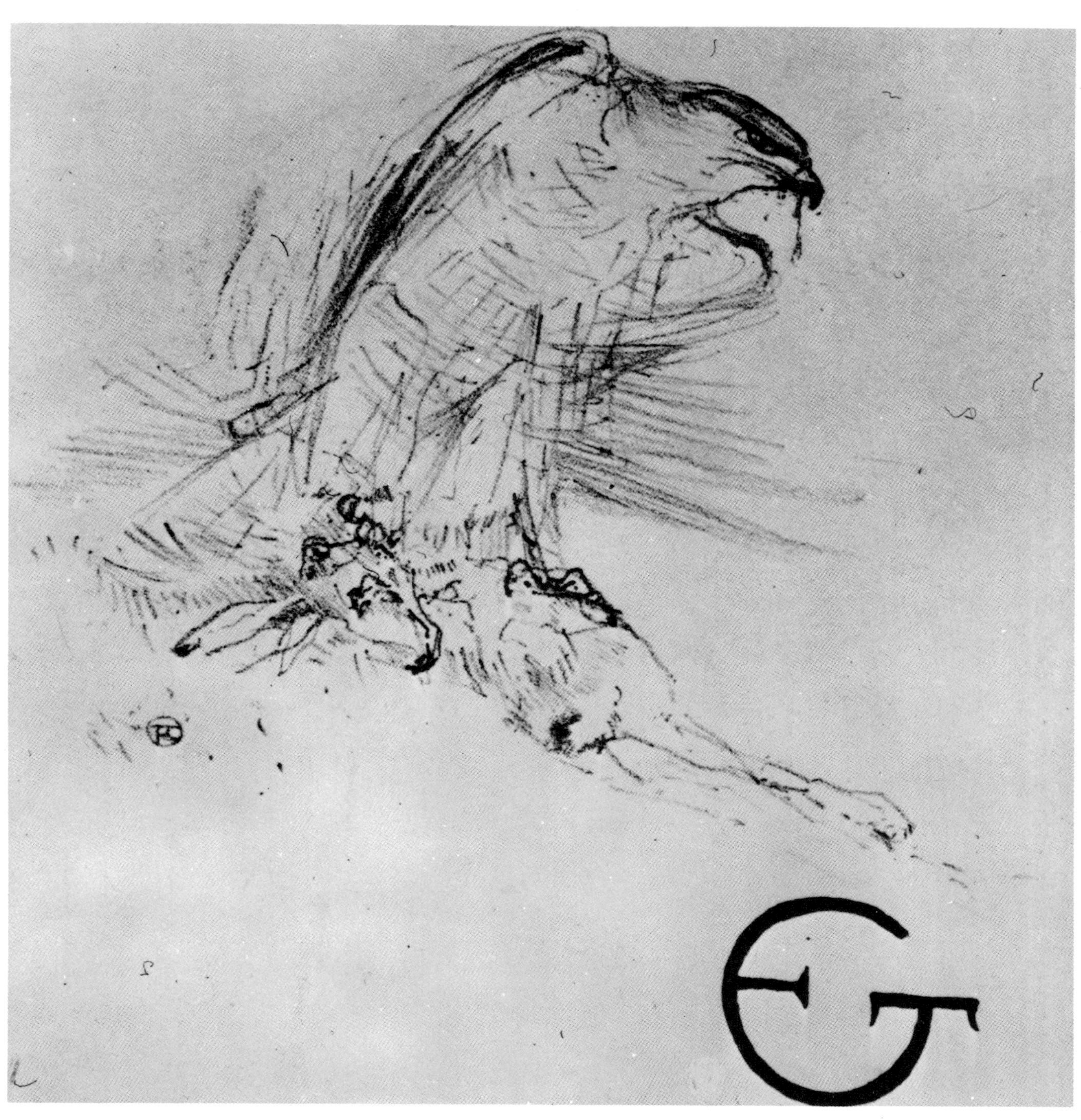

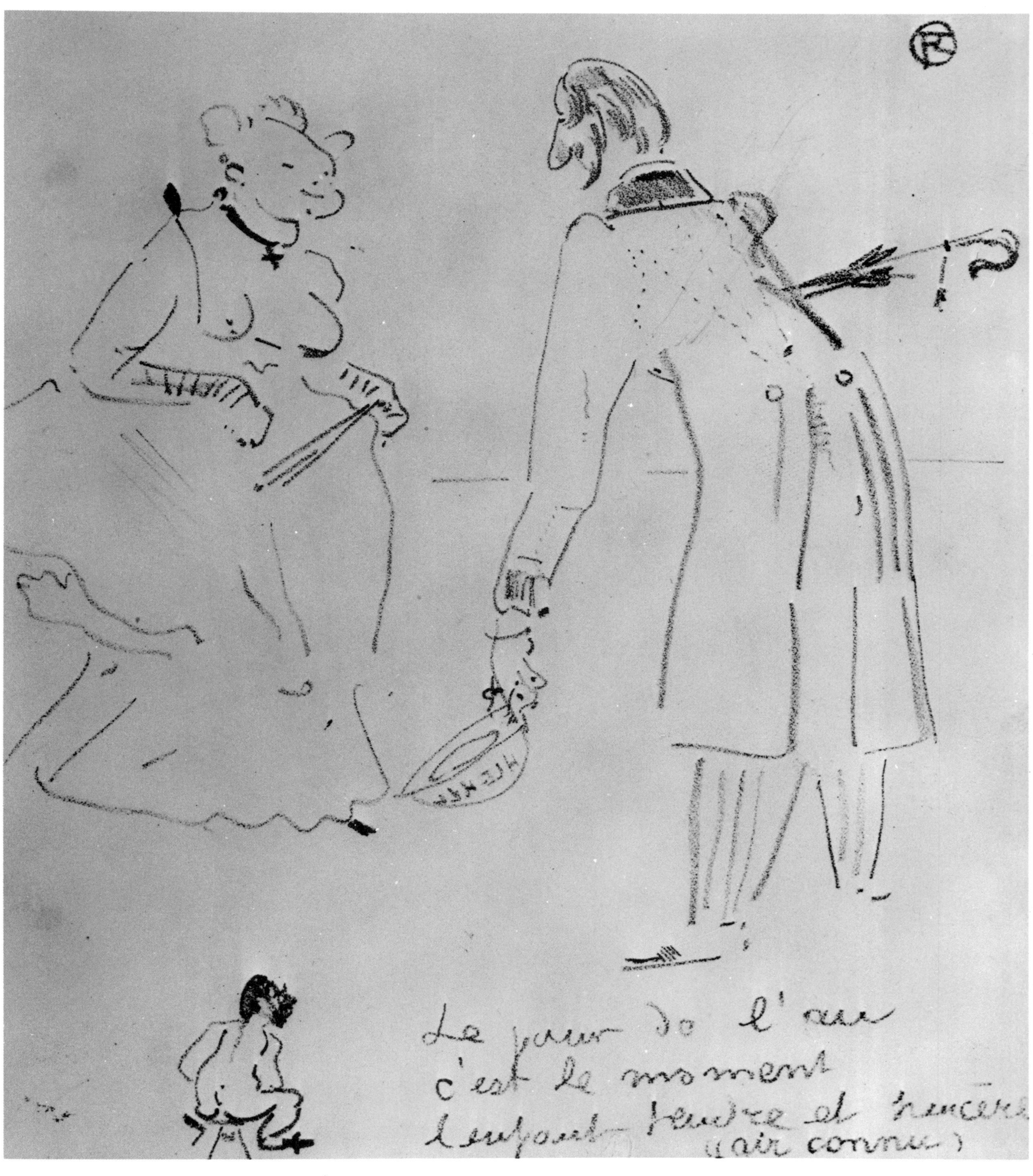
Le jour de l'an
c'est le moment
l'enfant tendre et sincère
(air connu)

275

276

279

280

281

282

Henri de Toulouse Lautrec vous prie
de lui faire l'honneur de visiter
le avril ses tableaux partant
pour Londres de 12. à 5 heures
14 avenue Frochot

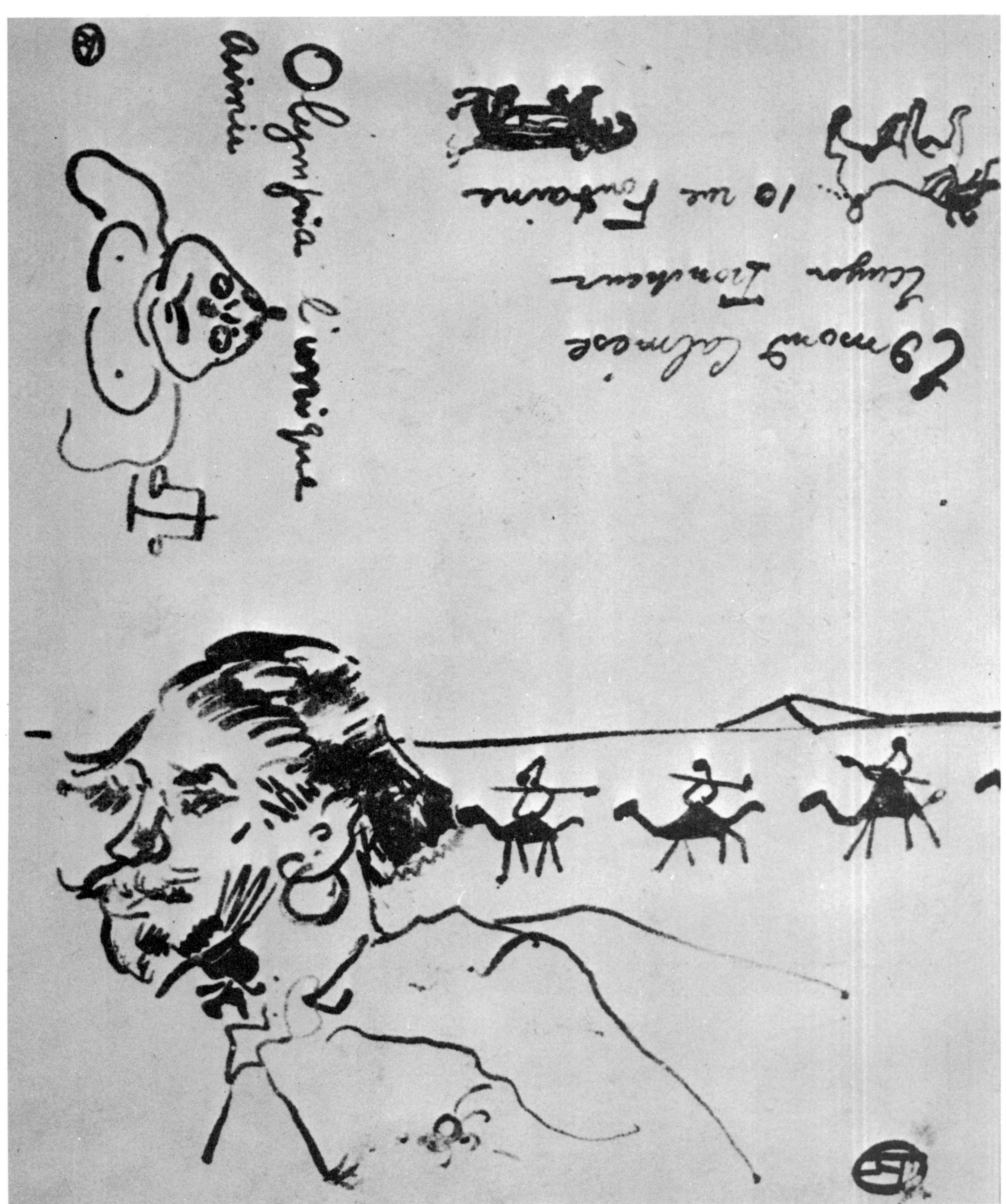
Olympia l'unique aimée
10 rue Fontaine

Men

PAUL LECLERCQ

Anglaise au café concert

Yvette Guilbert

Drawn by

H. de Toulouse Lautrec

Yvette Guilbert

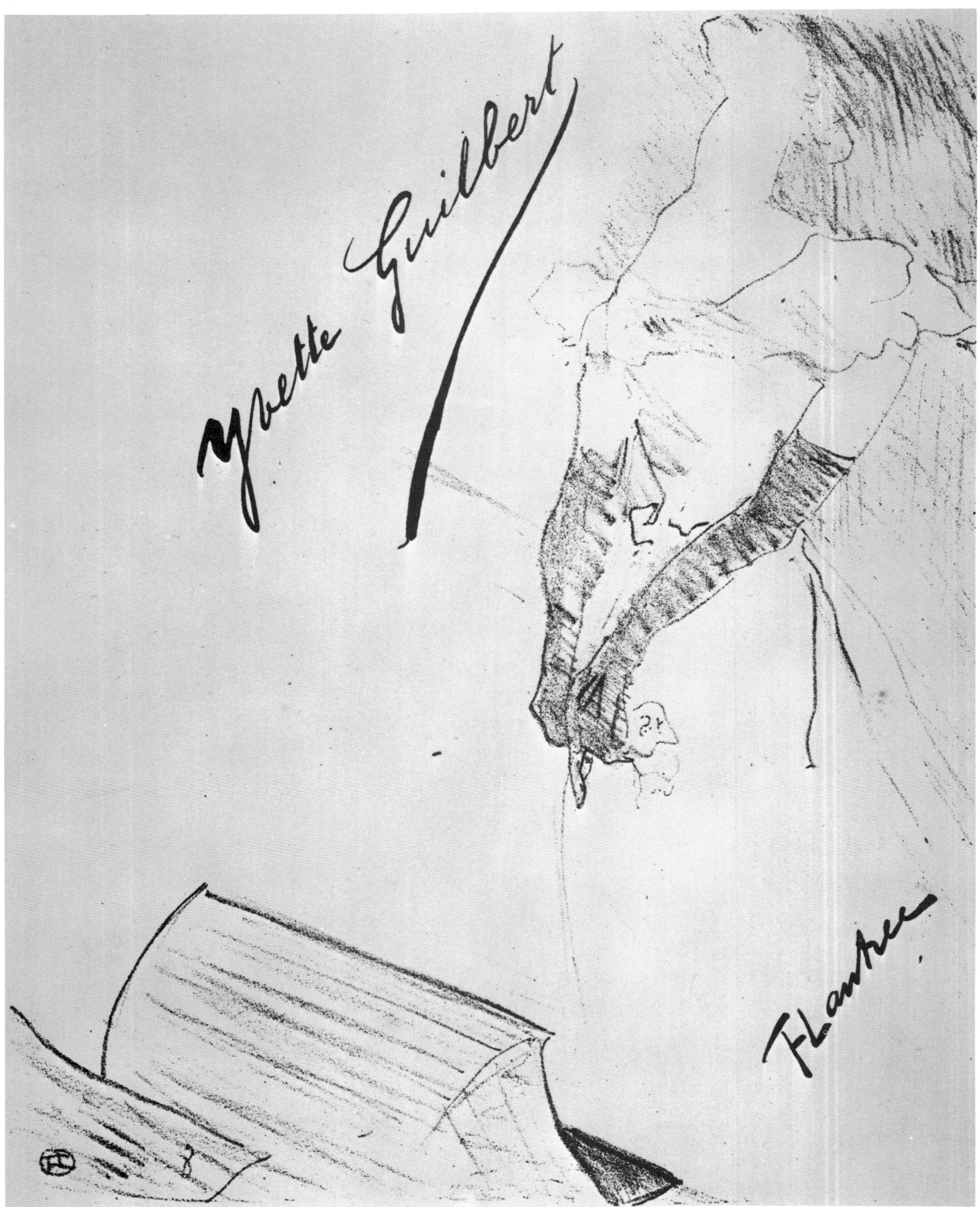
Yvette Guilbert

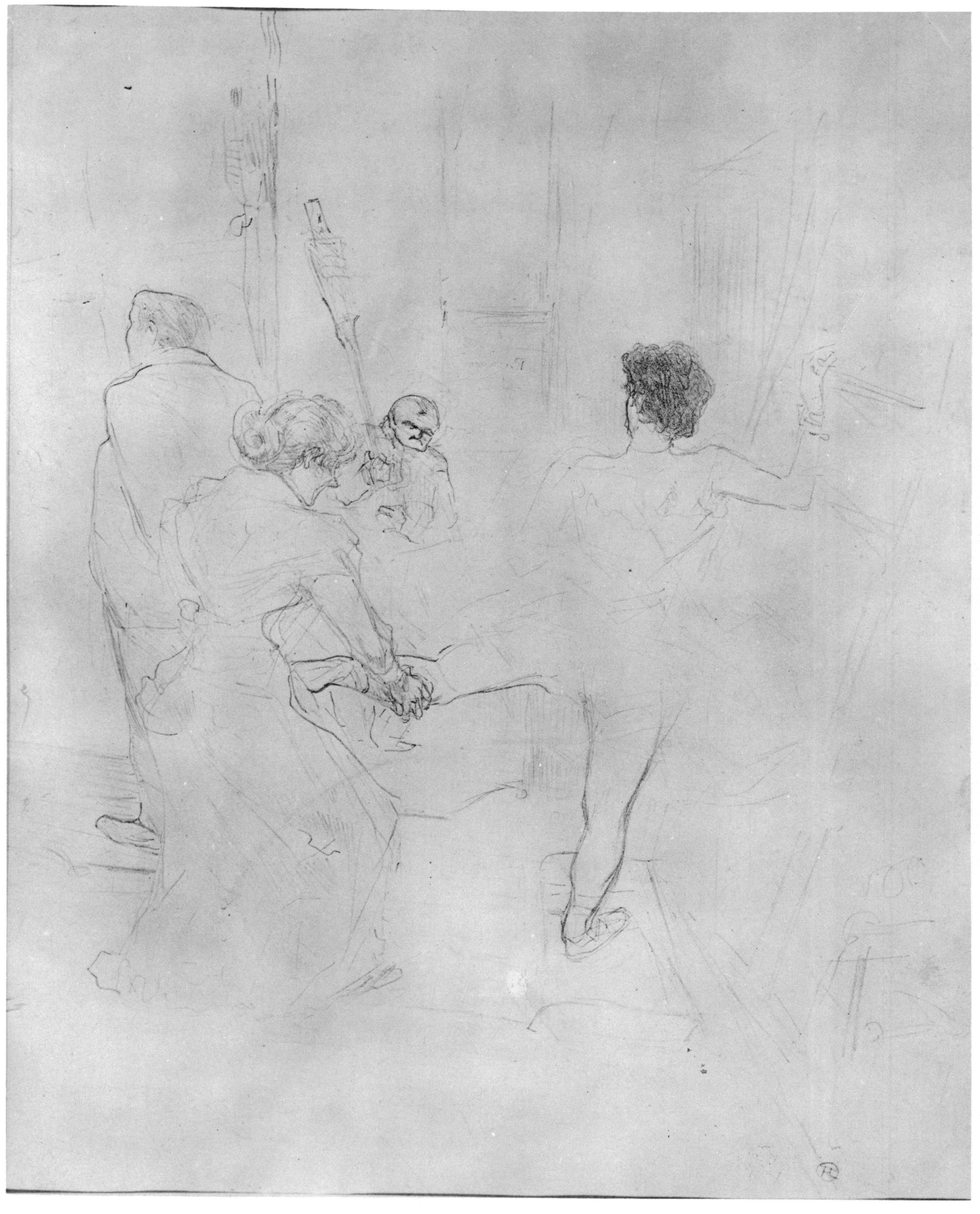

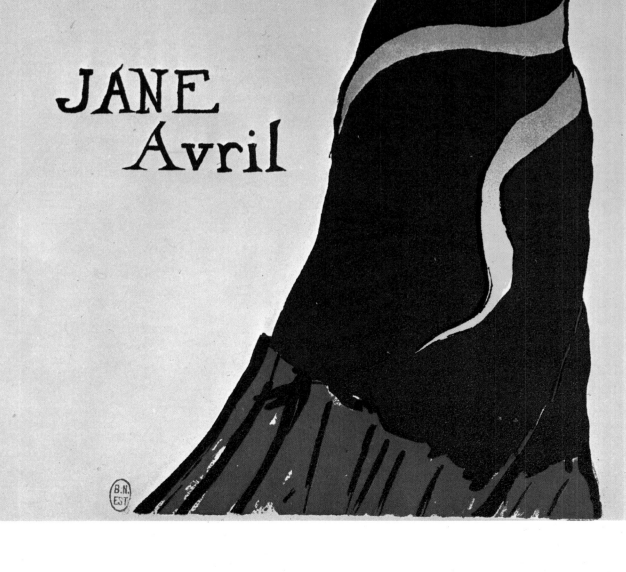

JANE
Avril

H. Stern, Paris.

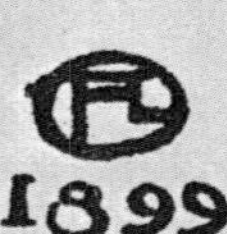

Dans le monde

331

332

Histoires
Naturelles

Coqs

La Pintade

La Dinde

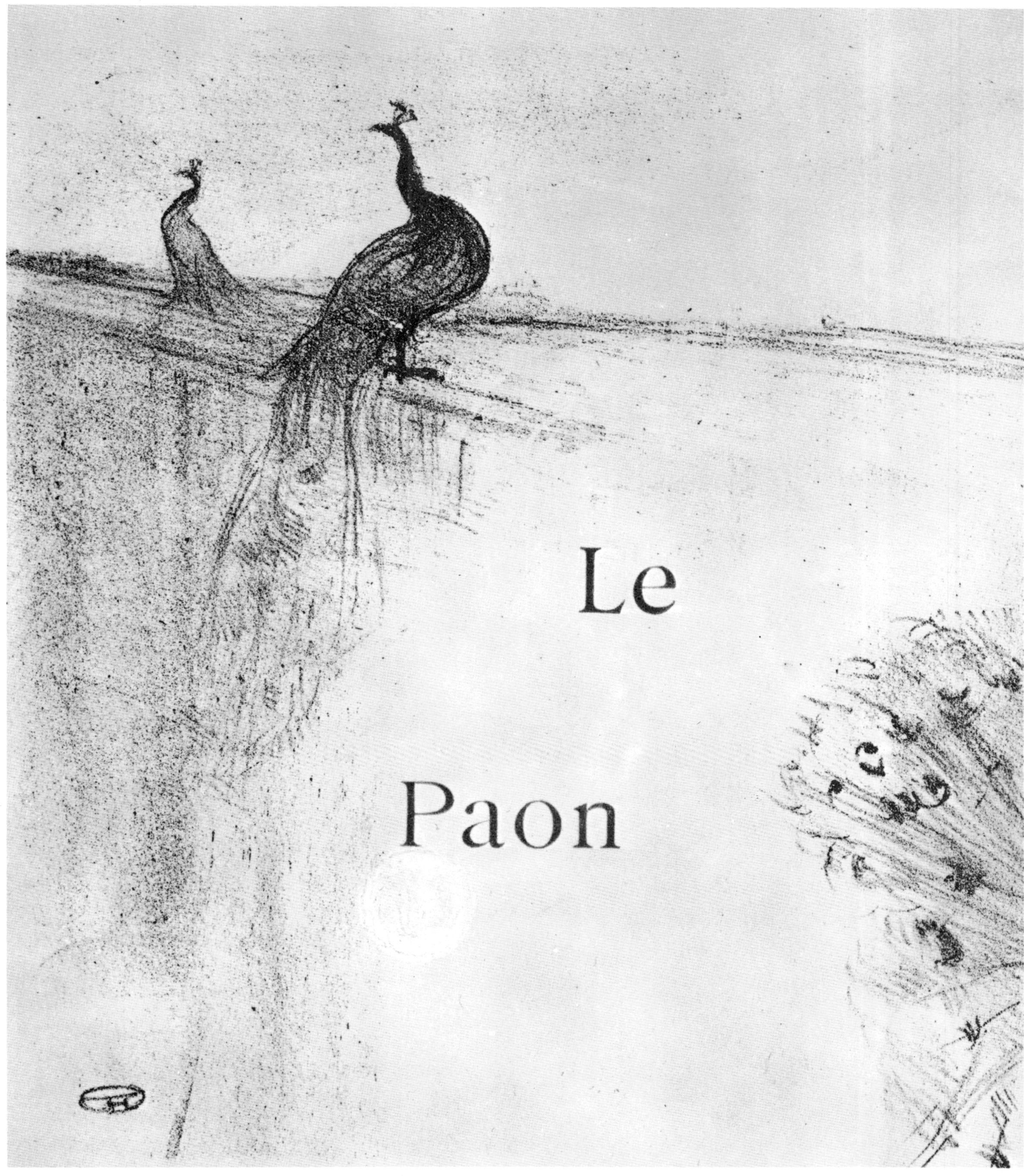
Le
Paon

Le
Cygne

Canards

Les Pigeons

L'Epervier

L'Escargot

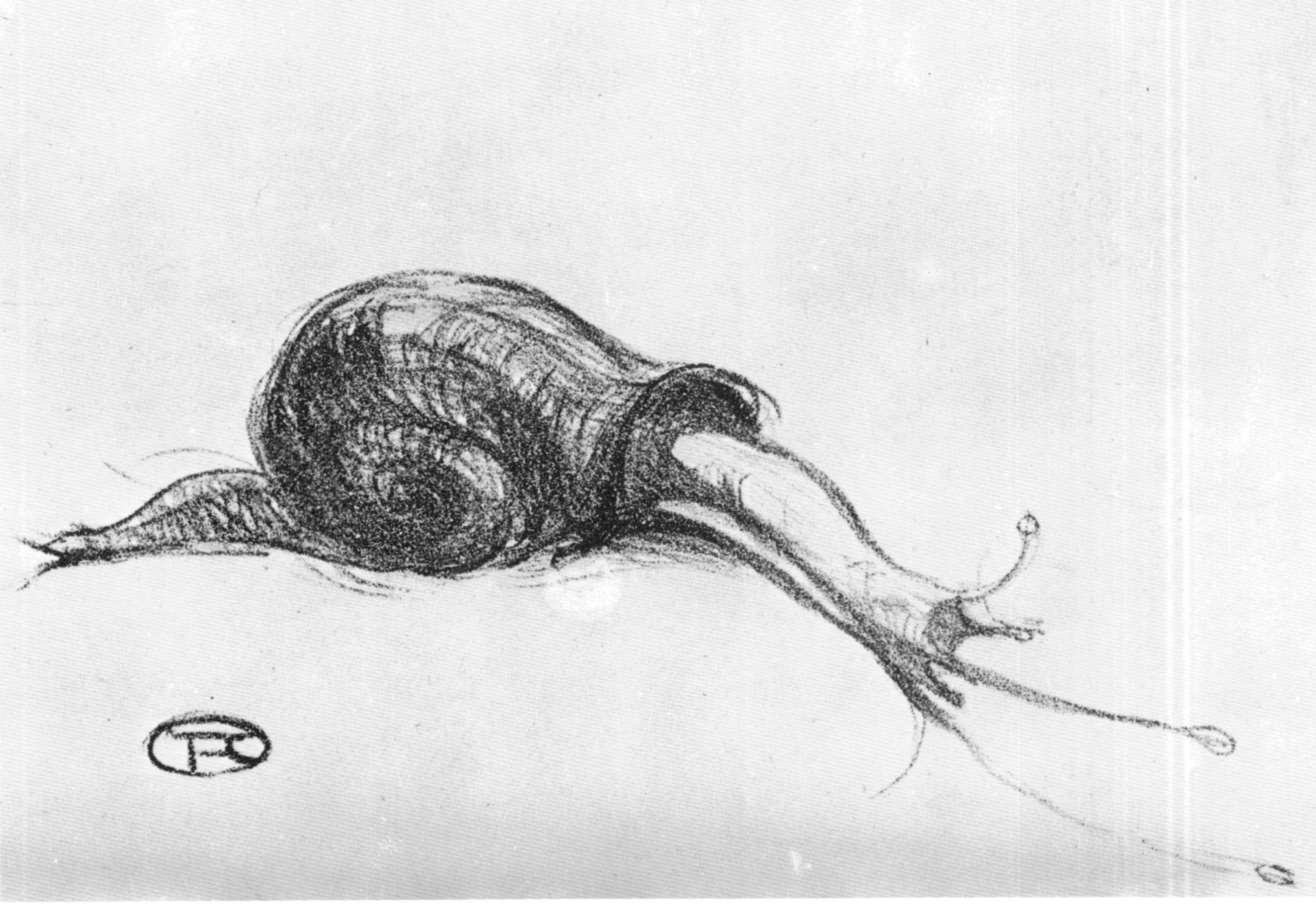

La Souris

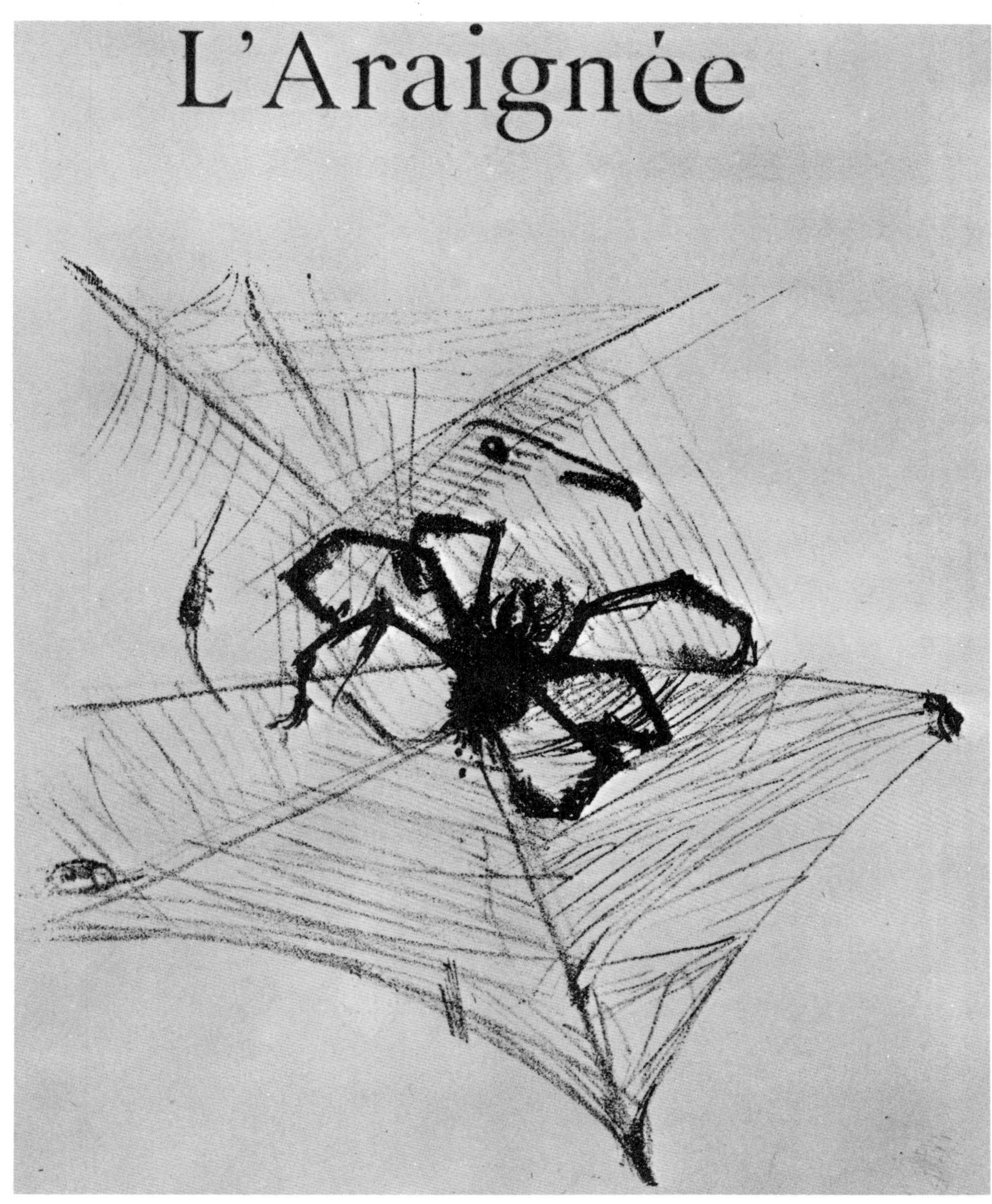
L'Araignée

Le Crapaud

Le Chien

Les
Lapins

Le Cerf

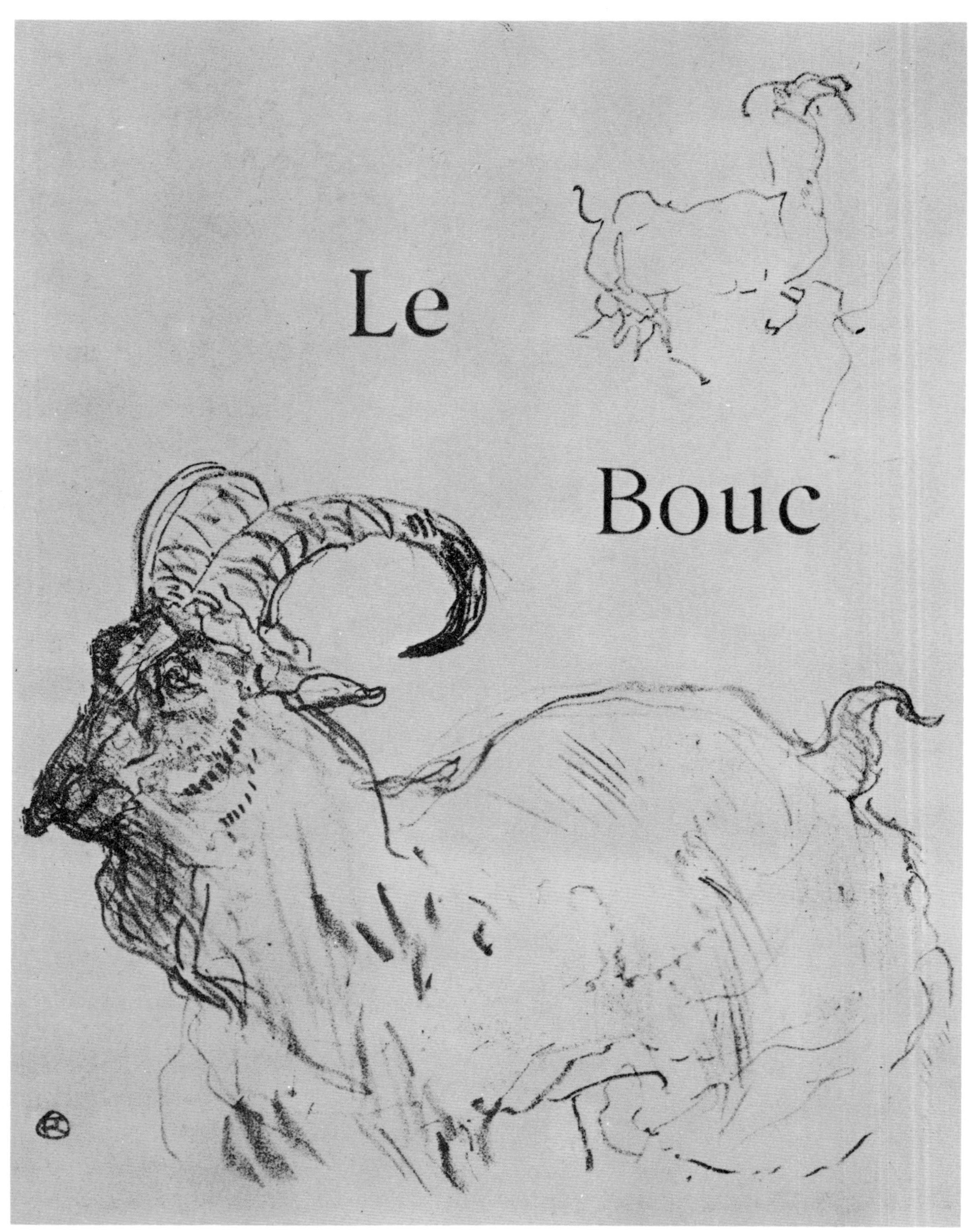
Le
Bouc

Les
Moutons

Le Taureau

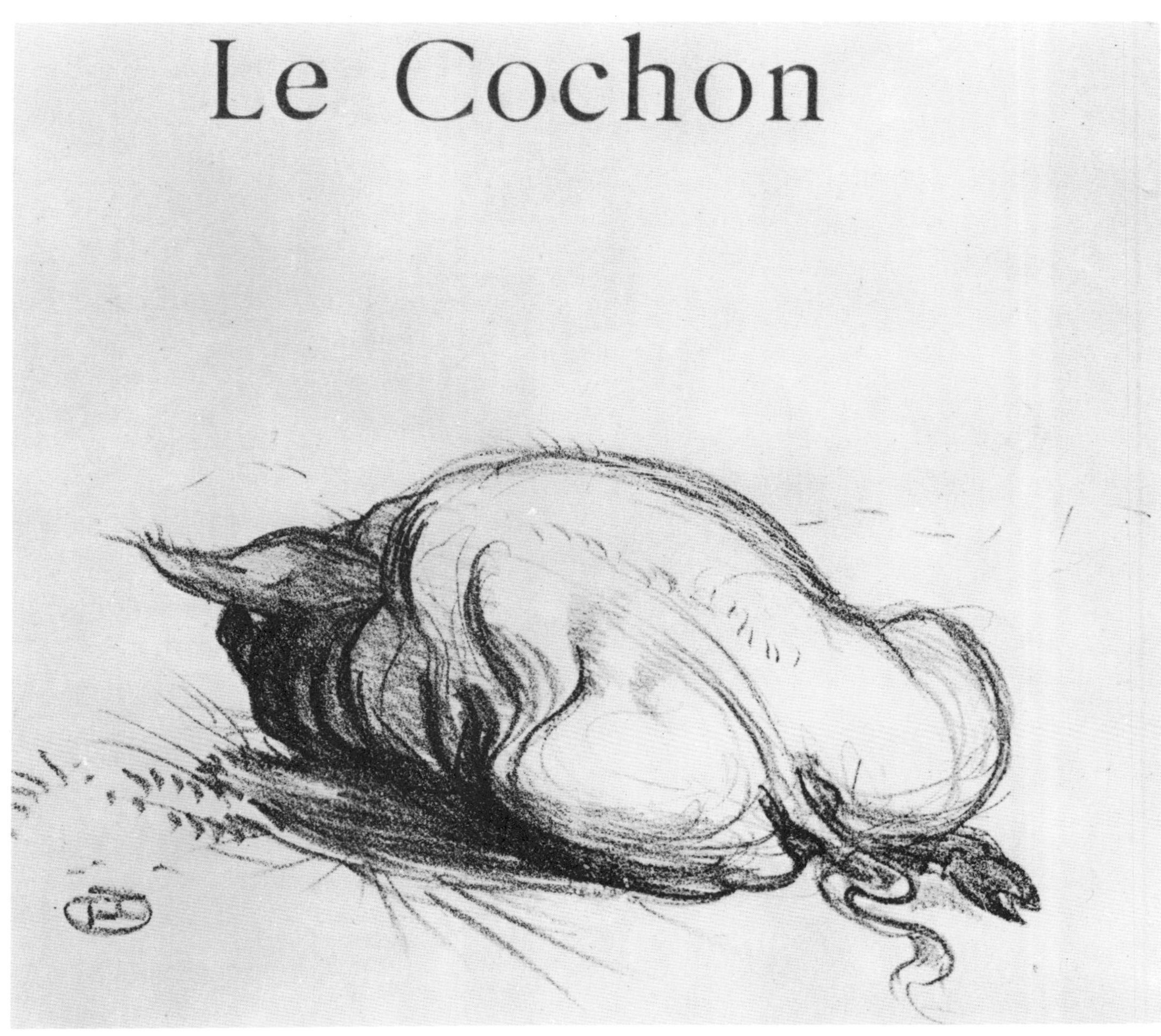
Le Cochon

Le
Cheval

Théâtre
Antoine
La Gitane
de
Richepin
Imp. EUGÈNE VERNEAU, 108, Rue Folie Méricourt. PARIS

LIST OF PLATES

◄ *Please fold out*

1891

1. LA GOULUE AU MOULIN ROUGE, coloured poster, 1,950 × 1,220 mm ($76^3/_4$ × 48 in.) (L.D. 339). Dresden Museum. Valentin-le-Désossé (1843–1907) was forty-seven years old when Lautrec drew him. His real name was Edme-Etienne Renaudin, and he came from a family of lawyers. He was supposed to be either a cashier or a bar-keeper by day, and a dancer at the Moulin Rouge in the evenings. He had led the waltz at the Tivoli Vauxhall, and had been dancer-in-chief at the Elysée-Montmartre. (See his interview in *L'Éclair*, 29 December 1902). Lautrec took as much interest in him as in La Goulue. In order to clarify Lautrec's relations with his models I asked Paul Leclercq if Lautrec spoke to Valentin when he met him, riding a donkey in the Bois de Boulogne. 'In the daytime, we did not greet him, and he did not solicit recognition,' Leclercq replied.
It is not generally realized that La Goulue's career as a dancer was nearly over when she appeared at the Moulin Rouge. Despite her success, she stayed there only for a brief period. By 7 February 1892, *Fin de Siècle* was already announcing that the Moulin Rouge 'has a monopoly on gay groups of dancing fools who know how to kick a leg', and that new débuts were taking place there every night, the latest attraction being 'a high-class demi-mondaine who wears a velvet mask'.
Mme Bodelsen knows three versions of this poster, each with different lettering.

1892

2. AU MOULIN ROUGE, LA GOULUE ET LA MÔME FROMAGE, incorrectly called *La Goulue et sa sœur*, coloured lithograph, 458 × 347 mm ($18^1/_{16}$ × $13^{11}/_{16}$ in.) (L.D. 11).
In 1891, *Paris-Distraction* gave an account of La Môme Fromage, who was the youngest member of a couturier's workshop. She had met La Goulue at the Elysée-Montmartre, and they 'went through life together, hardly ever leaving each other'. It was Sagot's opinion that Grille d'Egout rather than La Môme Fromage was shown in this lithograph.

3. L'ANGLAIS WARNER AU MOULIN ROUGE, entitled *Flirt* by Lautrec and *Rencontre au Moulin Rouge* by print-dealers, coloured lithograph, 470 × 372 mm ($18^1/_2$ × $14^5/_8$ in.) (L.D. 12).
Sagot kept this Englishman's name in his records. W. T. Warner was an impresario for the small theatres.
One hundred copies of this lithograph were printed on vellum by the Ancourt firm for Boussod.

4. LE PENDU (THE HANGED MAN), coloured poster printed without lettering, 700 × 468 mm ($27^9/_{16}$ × $18^7/_{16}$ in.) (L.D. 340). Dresden Museum.
This poster on the Calas affair was done in Toulouse for *La Dépêche*, which had commissioned it. Only thirty copies of it are supposed to have been printed in 1892 and thirty more in 1895, apart from the edition of the poster which was used for advertisement.
Mme Bodelsen points out that there were two different printings in 1892 and 1895, done on different stones, the second printing larger than the first.

5. REINE DE JOIE, coloured bookshop poster, 1,300 × 895 mm ($51^3/_{16}$ × $35^1/_4$ in.) (L.D. 342).
On 4 June, *Fin de Siècle* announced 'Lautrec's very original composition', which had just come out. The book itself, with a cover by Bonnard, was mentioned on 8 June.
Joyant speaks of a charcoal sketch at Albi, measuring 1,500 × 1,005 mm, ($59^1/_{16}$ × $39^9/_{16}$ in.) as well as a colour experiment done on the lithographic line.

6. BRUANT AUX AMBASSADEURS, coloured poster, 1,370 × 950 mm ($53^{15}/_{16}$ × $37^3/_8$ in.) (L.D. 343).
This poster is mentioned in *En Dehors*, 10 July 1892.

7. BRUANT À L'ELDORADO, coloured poster, 1,410 × 970 mm ($55^1/_2$ × $38^3/_{16}$ in.) (L.D. 344).
This poster is the reverse of the preceding one. Dresden Museum.

8. MISS LOIE FULLER, black and white lithograph, 430 × 270 mm ($16^{15}/_{16}$ × $10^{5}/_{8}$ in.) (L.D. 39). Printing of 50 copies, coloured by the artist. Published by Marty.

9. CONFETTI, coloured poster, 545 × 390 mm ($21^{7}/_{16}$ × $15^{3}/_{8}$ in.) (L.D. 352). Delteil dated this poster 1894, whereas Joyant dated the sketches for it 1893, and pointed out that it was reproduced in the February 1893 supplement of *L'Echo de Paris*. A painted sketch of it was dated 1894 by Lautrec.

10. L'ESTAMPE ORIGINALE (Cover for the magazine), coloured lithograph, 565 × 640 mm ($22^{1}/_{4}$ × $25^{3}/_{16}$ in.) (L.D. 17). In the first issue, dated January–March. Along with Lautrec's portrait by Maurin, works by Anquetin, Emile Bernard, Denis, Roussel, Vallotton and Ibels were also included.
Sagot owned an unfolded copy, which he considered 'very rare, probable unique', signed by Lautrec; he was asking 60 francs for it in 1903.

11. LE DIVAN JAPONAIS, coloured poster, 795 × 595 mm ($31^{5}/_{16}$ × $23^{7}/_{16}$ in.) (L.D. 341). Delteil dated this poster 1892, but the establishment did not open until the spring of 1893. In the poster can be seen Jane Avril; the Wagnerian music critic, Dujardin; and Yvette Guilbert. The poster is mentioned in *Le Père Peinard* on 30 April 1893.
M. Paul Prouté knows of two forgeries derived from the poster.

12. JANE AVRIL AU JARDIN DE PARIS, coloured poster, 1,300 × 940 mm ($51^{3}/_{16}$ × 37 in.) (L.D. 345), first state, before lettering. The second state (3 June) has 'Jardin de Paris' written on it in black.
Registered 8 May 1893 by Chaix. *Le Triboulet* spoke about the opening of the Jardin de Paris on 7 May, saying 'There isn't a pleasanter place in Paris.'
As can be seen, Joyant was wrong to give July 1893 as the date of Jane Avril's début in the music-hall.

13. CAUDIEUX, coloured poster, 1,206 × 905 mm ($47^{1}/_{2}$ × $35^{5}/_{8}$ in.) (L.D. 346).

14. AU PIED DE L'ÉCHAFAUD (AT THE FOOT OF THE SCAFFOLD), coloured poster, 820 × 580 mm ($32^{5}/_{16}$ × $22^{13}/_{16}$ in.) (L.D. 347), first state. The second bears the title 'Au pied...'
For the 'Mémoires de l'abbé Faure', almoner at the prison of La Roquette, which appeared in *Le Matin*.

15. BRUANT DANS SON CABARET, coloured poster, 1,270 × 925 mm (50 × $36^{7}/_{16}$ in.) (L.D. 348), first state, that of Delteil; second state has the title 'Aristide Bruant'; third state has the words 'Le Chansonnier de Montmartre', a monthly review; fourth state, second of Delteil, with the title erased; fifth state has 'Alcazar lyrique' on the top left-hand corner.

16. A SAINT-LAZARE, song-title, 240 × 160 mm ($9^{7}/_{16}$ × $6^{5}/_{16}$ in.) (L.D. 10). Signed 'Tréclau'. It was reproduced in the magazine *Le Mirliton*, No. 39, 1 August 1887. There is a sketch of it on Gillot paper at the Albi Museum.

17. LA MODISTE DRESSANT UN CHAPEAU (THE MILLINER TRIMMING A HAT), menu for the 23 June 1893 dinner given by the Société des Indépendants. Lithograph in two tints, 300 × 210 mm ($11^{13}/_{16}$ × $8^{1}/_{4}$ in.) (L.D. 13).
There is one state before lettering (150 copies printed) and one after lettering, reproduced here, which was used as the menu.
The milliner, Renée Vert, was the fiancée of Adolphe Albert, a friend of Lautrec's. According to Natanson, 'Hats delighted him as much as they did Renoir... he couldn't stop himself from stroking muffs and dresses as though they were human beings.'

18. LE PETIT TROTTIN (THE LITTLE ERRAND-GIRL), song-title, music by Dihau, 280 × 200 mm (11 × $7^{7}/_{8}$ in.) (L.D. 27), Delteil's first state (the second state adds the name and address of the publisher).
Sagot knew of thirty copies of this lithograph before lettering.
Other people in Lautrec's milieu had used the same theme before him; see 'Les Petits Trottins, words by Baillot, designs by Balluriau' (*Fin de Siècle*, 14 May 1892). Sketches for this piece at Albi were wrongly dated 1894 by Joyant. *La Vie Parisienne* spoke of the errand-girls in the following way on 1 January 1898: 'They're young, fresh and cheaply

dressed, but their badly-shod little feet... will kick high enough to break down the resistance of every monocle.' At the same time, the newspaper *Grand Guignol* (15 January 1898) published some sentimental verses by Thomas Chesnois on the errand-girls.

'Souvent ils sont en butte
A des propos très libertins,
Mais ce sont de sages trottins,
Ils ne font pas la culbute,
Les jolis trottins de la Butte.'

(They're often the prey
Of some very indecent propositions
But they're good girls,
They don't take the plunge,
The pretty errand-girls of Montmartre.)

19. COVER-TITLE PAGE FOR 'VIEILLES HISTOIRES', poems by Jean Goudey, known as Goudezki, with music by Désiré Dihau, published by Ondet, 340 × 520 mm ($13^3/_8 \times 20^1/_2$ in.) (L.D. 18), third state.
Lautrec illustrated some of the *Vieilles Histoires*, and the rest were done by his friends Rachou and Ibels.
The proofs before lettering (100 copies were printed, 40 of them coloured) were sold at Kleinmann, and also at Ondet, who announced in *Le Bottin* in 1897 that he still had some in his possession (this lot was bought up a little later by M. Paul Prouté.)
Goudezki would sing his songs in a deep, solemn voice that was irresistibly funny (see the description, given by *Fin de Siècle* on 17 February 1892, of a party at which he sang). The first state is before lettering, the second before the two lines were drawn in the bottom left-hand corner.

20. POUR TOI (FOR YOU), Plate 2 of *Vieilles Histoires*, 270 × 196 mm ($10^5/_8 \times 7^3/_4$ in.) (L.D. 19), one of 100 proofs of the first state before lettering (the second state is with lettering); the second state before lettering contains the mark of Floury (L.D. 19, 22, 24 and 25), on heavy paper (Japan and vellum), reserved for buyers of luxury prints at Joyant's.

21. NUIT BLANCHE (WHITE NIGHT), Plate 4 of *Vieilles Histoires*, 257 × 170 mm ($10^1/_8 \times 6^{11}/_{16}$ in.) (L.D. 20), first of two states.

22. ULTIME BALLADE (LAST BALLAD), Plate 9 of *Vieilles Histoires*, 265 × 180 mm ($10^7/_{16} \times 7^1/_{16}$ in.) (L.D. 23), first of two states.

23. SAGESSE (WISDOM), Plate 8 of *Vieilles Histoires*, 254 × 180 mm (10 × $7^1/_{16}$ in.) (L.D. 22), first state.

24. CARNOT MALADE! (CARNOT ILL), a song sung at the Chat Noir, brought out by Ondet in October(?) 1893, 239 × 175 mm ($9^7/_{16} \times 6^7/_8$ in.) (L.D. 25); the first state was unknown to Delteil (who knew of two) without the folds in the curtain. President Sadi Carnot had had a liver attack during the summer of 1893, and had gone to Marly for treatment. The small newspapers had made fun of this; *Le Triboulet* (27 August), referring to the president's notorious thinness, had said, 'M. Carnot has a stomach. Until now, no one had noticed the fact.'

25. TA BOUCHE (YOUR MOUTH), Plate 5 of *Vieilles Histoires*, 250 × 182 mm ($9^{13}/_{16} \times 7^3/_{16}$ in.) (L.D. 21), first state of two, before lettering.
There are some proofs in sepia, in greenish tints, and coloured.

26. ÉTUDE DE FEMME (STUDY OF A WOMAN), title-page of a tune by Hector Sombre arranged by D. Dihau, 250 × 190 mm ($9^7/_8 \times 7^1/_2$ in.) (L.D. 24), first state before lettering.
Joyant mentions a painted sketch of this study.

27. PAUVRE PIERREUSE (POOR STREET-WALKER), title-page of a song from the repertory of Eugénie Buffet, 210 × 170 mm ($8^1/_4 \times 6^{11}/_{16}$ in.) (L.D. 26), third impression with different lettering (there are two states, before and after lettering). There are some copies without lettering that were printed at a later date, and which show a difference in the edge of the woman's hand.

28. JANE AVRIL, first plate in the *Café-Concert* series, 265 × 213 mm ($10^{7}/_{16} \times 8^{3}/_{8}$ in.) (L.D. 28), first state. Three states, according to M. Paul Prouté: one without text, which is in the album; a second with the words 'répertoire Jane Avril' and Bosc's address; a third with the text erased, and the black globe in the upper left-hand corner missing.

29. YVETTE GUILBERT, same series, 249 × 190 mm ($9^{13}/_{16} \times 7^{1}/_{2}$ in.) (L.D. 29), first state.
Yvette was then playing at the Scala. One could see the tormented mask of her face, the haunting eyes.

30. PAULA BRÉBION, same series, 260 × 190 mm ($10^{1}/_{4} \times 7^{1}/_{2}$ in.) (L.D. 30).
A singer at the Scala with a lisping voice.

31. MARY HAMILTON, same series, 268 × 170 mm ($10^{9}/_{16} \times 6^{11}/_{16}$ in.) (L.D. 31). A very small printing.
An English transvestite *diseuse*. Exhibited at the Brussels *Libre Esthétique* in 1895, under the title *The Fair Miss H.* There exists a reprint by Frapier, done in 1925.

32. EDMÉE LESCOT, EN DANSEUSE ESPAGNOLE (EDMÉE LESCOT AS A SPANISH DANCER), same series, 268 × 178 mm ($19^{9}/_{16} \times 7$ in.) (L.D. 32).
Seen at Les Ambassadeurs.

33. LE PÈRE DUCARRE AUX AMBASSADEURS, same series, 259 × 195 mm ($10^{3}/_{16} \times 7^{11}/_{16}$ in.) (L.D. 36).
Pierre Ducarre was described in the *Courrier Français* on 7 June 1891, with his salt-and-pepper hair, and his thick beard cut in the shape of a horse-shoe. After being the manager of the Bal Valentino, he had the idea of opening a café-concert in the Champs-Elysées, Les Ambassadeurs.

34. COMIQUE EXCENTRIQUE ANGLAIS (ECCENTRIC ENGLISH COMEDIAN), same series, 333 × 200 mm ($13^{7}/_{8} \times 7^{7}/_{8}$ in.) (L.D. 38).
The singer Libert, according to Astre. Sagot calls this *Chanteur Américain.*

35. MADAME ABDALA EN BÉBÉ (MADAME ABDALA AS A BABY), same series, 270 × 197 mm ($10^{5}/_{8} \times 7^{3}/_{4}$ in.) (L.D. 33).
Montorgueil says that she deliberately distorted her face. She played at the Scala.

36. CAUDIEUX DANSANT AU PETIT CASINO (CAUDIEUX DANCING AT THE PETIT CASINO), same series, 270 × 211 mm ($10^{5}/_{8} \times 8^{5}/_{16}$ in.) (L.D. 35).

37. UNE SPECTATRICE PENDANT LA CHANSON DE POLIN (A WOMAN IN THE AUDIENCE DURING POLIN'S SONG), same series, 265 × 182 mm ($10^{7}/_{16} \times 7^{3}/_{16}$ in.) (L.D. 37).

38. ARISTIDE BRUANT, same series, 265 × 208 mm ($10^{7}/_{16} \times 8^{3}/_{16}$ in.) (L.D. 34).
Probably at Les Ambassadeurs.

39. JUDIC ET DIHAU, OU L'ESSAI DU CORSET (JUDIC AND DIHAU, OR TRYING ON A CORSET), published by Kleinmann, 367 × 260 mm) ($14^{7}/_{16} \times 10^{1}/_{4}$ in.) (L.D. 56); printing of 100 copies, plus some on Japanese vellum.
Reproduced on Gillot paper in *L'Escarmouche*, 10 December.

40. PROGRAMME FOR 'UNE FAILLITE', 321 × 239 mm ($12^{5}/_{8} \times 9^{7}/_{16}$ in.) (L.D. 14), first state of two, before lettering.
The play opened on 8 November.

41. ANTOINE AND GÉMIER IN 'UNE FAILLITE', 295 × 365 mm ($11^{5}/_{8} \times 14^{3}/_{8}$ in.) (L.D. 63); 50 copies printed.
Delteil wrongly dated this work 1894. It was printed in black and in green.

42. FANTAISIE DE CARNAVAL, two people in fancy-dress, 250 × 160 mm ($9^{13}/_{16} \times 6^{5}/_{16}$ in.) (L.D. 64), second state.
There are two states: the first before lettering in successive printings, the mouth white at first, then red; the second printed without a border, in the June (not March) 1894 issue of *La Revue Blanche*, and with the complete subject in the *Album de la Revue Blanche* of 1895.
There is one proof printed on the back of *Antigone*. Therefore, this work dates from November 1893 and not from March 1894, as Delteil claimed.
Natanson speaks of Lautrec's delight at having obtained another stone 'simply for the double accent of red that parts the lips of one of the subjects'.

43. POURQUOI PAS?... (WHY NOT?...), 364 × 267 mm ($14^{5}/_{16}$ × $10^{1}/_{2}$ in.) (L.D. 40). There exist some proofs in green. This work, and all the others which came out in *L'Escarmouche*, were merely reproduced in the newspaper. A printing of 100 was made of all these works beforehand. Reproduced in *L'Escarmouche* on 12 November.

44. AUX VARIÉTÉS, MLLE LENDER AND BRASSEUR, 340 × 240 mm ($13^{3}/_{8}$ × $9^{7}/_{16}$ in.) (L.D. 41).
Reproduced in *L'Escarmouche* on 19 November.
First appearance of Marcelle Lender, who was to play a major role the following year.

45. EN QUARANTE, 280 × 230 mm (11 × $9^{1}/_{16}$ in.) (L.D. 42).
Reproduced in *L'Escarmouche* on 26 November.

46. LENDER AND BARON, 325 × 235 mm ($12^{13}/_{16}$ × $9^{1}/_{4}$ in.) (L.D. 43).
Reproduced in *L'Escarmouche* on 3 December.

47. RÉPÉTITION GÉNÉRALE AUX FOLIES-BERGÈRE (DRESS REHEARSAL AT THE FOLIES-BERGÈRE), 370 × 250 mm ($14^{9}/_{16}$ × $9^{13}/_{16}$ in.) (L.D. 44).
Reproduced in *L'Escarmouche* on 3 December.
Emilienne d'Alençon is being shown here how to dance by Mariquita of the Opéra.
There are some copies containing attempts at colouring.

48. AU MOULIN ROUGE, UN RUDE, UN VRAI RUDE, 320 × 250 mm ($12^{5}/_{8}$ × $9^{13}/_{16}$ in.) (L.D. 45).
Reproduced in *L'Escarmouche* on 10 December, 1893.
At the center, we seem to recognize not Lautrec's father but the engraver Boetzel, and to the right, the painter Joseph Albert. Commentators have been surprised by the title: some thought that the word *rude* (uncouth) was an ironic reference to Lautrec's father who, according to his son, 'could have a spree on nothing but café-au-lait.' Others thought of the sculptor Rude, on whom R. Duguet had just written a book: the men would seem to be persuading the young woman that she looked like a sculpture by Rude, in order to amuse themselves by hearing her boast of it everywhere. This idea could be linked with two caricatures by Métivet which had been published in *Le Rire*: 'A young woman is asserting that she has "pear-shaped buttocks just like La Giaconda", and an Italian is showing his noble bearing by announcing, "I posed for the legs of Mister Rodin's Balzac" (whose legs are hidden by a dressing-gown)'. Lapparent (*op. cit.*, p. 6) had a somewhat similar notion: 'The count of Toulouse-Lautrec ridiculous? On the contrary, an extremely dashing gentleman. His son shows him smoothing his beard with such a statuesque gesture that people cried out, "A Rude! An authentic Rude!"' Actually, the 'rude' in question is merely a glass of pure wine. This can be seen by re-reading *Madame Sans-Gêne* (played in 1893): the heroine says about tea, 'You don't fancy this hot water? Would you rather have some *rude*?'
There is a sketch for this lithograph in the Albi Museum.

49. AUX FOLIES-BERGÈRE, LES PUDEURS DE M. PRUDHOMME (THE MODESTY OF M. PRUDHOMME), 370 × 220 mm ($14^{9}/_{16}$ × $8^{11}/_{16}$ in.) (L.D. 46).
Reproduced in *L'Escarmouche* on 17 December.

50. À LA RENAISSANCE, SARAH BERNHARDT IN 'PHÈDRE', 340 × 231 mm ($13^{3}/_{8}$ × $9^{1}/_{8}$ in.) (L.D. 47).
Reproduced in *L'Escarmouche* on 24 December.
It should be remembered that these were the performances in which Proust saw 'La Berma'.

51. À LA GAIETÉ-ROCHECHOUART, NICOLLE EN PIERREUSE (NICOLLE AS STREET-WALKER), 367 × 260 mm ($14^{7}/_{16}$ × $10^{1}/_{4}$ in.) (L.D. 48).
Reproduced in *L'Escarmouche* on 31 December. It must be one of the rejected pieces for the *Café-concert* series.

1894

52. ROSE CARON IN 'FAUST', lithograph reproduced in *L'Escarmouche* on 7 January 1894, 370 × 260 mm ($14^{9}/_{16}$ × $10^{1}/_{4}$ in.) (L.D. 49).

53. AU MOULIN-ROUGE, L'UNION FRANCO-RUSSE, lithograph reproduced in *L'Escarmouche* on 7 January 1894, 328 × 247 mm ($12^{15}/_{16}$ × $9^{3}/_{4}$ in.) (L.D. 50).

The young worker is carrying the newspaper *Paris-Sport* under his arm; this was the title given this work when memory of the Franco-Russian celebration had faded.

54. UNE REDOUTE AU MOULIN ROUGE (A GALA EVENING AT THE MOULIN ROUGE), 50 copies printed for Kleinmann, 297 × 430 mm ($11^{11}/_{16}$ × $16^{15}/_{16}$ in.) (L.D. 65).
One of the trial proofs which we know in black or in green. The two subjects of the previous lithograph appear in this one, with La Goulue riding on a donkey. Was it one of those galas described in *La Revue Blanche* (1893, II, p. 106), known as *analcades?* Or was it merely an excuse for showing us the entire Moulin Rouge troupe, as Chéret had done in his 1891 poster?

55. ANTOINE AND MME SAVILLE IN 'L'INQUIÉTUDE', by J. Perrin and C. Couturier, at the Théâtre Libre. This lithograph was reproduced in *L'Escarmouche* on 14 January 1894, 369 × 264 mm ($14^{1}/_{2}$ × $10^{3}/_{8}$ in.) (L.D. 51).

56. RÉJANE AND GALIPAUX IN 'MADAME SANS-GÊNE', 340 × 265 mm ($13^{3}/_{8}$ × $10^{7}/_{16}$ in.) (L.D. 52), one of 10 on Japanese vellum (80 were printed on plain vellum for Kleinmann).
This scene from *Madame Sans-Gêne* was unbelievably successful, although it was pointed out that Réjane 'exaggerates a bit'. Jules Lemaître saw nothing in it but 'a clumsier version of the scene with the dancing-master in *Le Bourgeois Gentilhomme*'. The lithograph was meant to be reproduced in *L'Escarmouche*, but the newspaper had gone out of business.

57. HEAD OF RÉJANE IN 'MADAME SANS-GÊNE', 288 × 221 mm ($11^{5}/_{16}$ × $8^{11}/_{16}$ in.) (L.D. 266).
For some reason, Delteil dated this work 1899, whereas Joyant dated the drawing 1894. Twelve copies were pulled from the plate, which was used again before, as well as after, it became the property of the Albi Museum.

58. HEAD OF POLAIRE, 342 × 222 mm ($13^{1}/_{2}$ × $8^{3}/_{4}$ in.) (L.D. 227); a printing of about ten copies.
Delteil dated this work 1898, but it should be linked to the previous one. The actual drawings for it were done in 1895, and they showed Polaire as she had appeared at Les Ambassadeurs around March 1894. (Cf. No. 175.)

59. BARTET AND MOUNET-SULLY IN 'ANTIGONE', 358 × 268 mm ($14^{1}/_{8}$ × $10^{9}/_{16}$ in.) (L.D. 53), first state of two. A lithograph that was intended for publication in *L'Escarmouche*, and which must date from the end of 1893.

60. LELOIR AND MORÉNO IN 'LES FEMMES SAVANTES', 375 × 263 mm ($14^{3}/_{4}$ × $10^{3}/_{8}$ in.) (L.D. 54). Lithograph done in September 1893, which Kleinmann brought out in February 1894. One of the surplus copies (a printing of 50).
The play was performed only on 26 August, 3 September and 18 September 1893. At that time Moréno, after striking successes at the Conservatoire, and a début which was not brilliant at the Comédie-Française, was beginning to be very popular because of her 'ravishing voice'.

61. L'ÉVANOUISSEMENT (THE FAINTING-SPELL), 375 × 279 mm ($14^{3}/_{4}$ × 11 in.) (L.D. 294). Only a few copies were printed. I have pointed out that this piece, published without a date by Delteil, ought to go with the following one, as it contains the same characters, in the same costumes, acting in the same play.

62. LUGNÉ-POË AND BALDY IN 'L'IMAGE', by Beaubourg, at the Théâtre de l'Œuvre, 312 × 228 mm ($12^{1}/_{4}$ × 9 in.) (L.D. 57), published by Kleinmann. One of the surplus copies (the edition numbered 50).

63. DEBLÈVE AND BALDY, wrongly cited as Lugné-Poë and Baldy, in *Au-dessus des Forces Humaines* by Bjoernson, 290 × 240 mm ($11^{7}/_{16}$ × $9^{7}/_{16}$ in.) (L.D. 55), published by Kleinmann.
It can be seen, in Lugné-Poë's *Acrobaties* (p. 72), that Lautrec portrayed Lugné-Poë's friend Deblève, known as Chevalier, in this lithograph.

64. BRANDÈS IN A BOX, 360 × 265 mm ($14^{3}/_{16}$ × $10^{7}/_{16}$ in.) (L.D. 60), surplus print (edition of 25).

65. BRANDÈS AND LE BARGY, IN THE THIRD ACT OF 'CABOTINS', by Pailleron, at the Comédie-Française, 420 × 330 mm ($16^{9}/_{16}$ × 13 in.) (L.D. 61). Kleinmann published 50 copies in green tints.

66. BRANDÈS AND LELOIR IN THE SECOND ACT OF 'CABOTINS', by Pailleron, at the Comédie-Française, 400 × 300 mm ($15^{3}/_{4}$ × $11^{3}/_{4}$ in.) (L.D. 62). Lithograph in green tints published by Kleinmann. Considered extremely rare, like the previous one.

67. BABYLONE D'ALLEMAGNE, reduced version of the following work for the book-jacket, 200 × 140 mm ($7^{7}/_{8} \times 5^{1}/_{2}$ in.) (L.D. 76), first state before lettering (there are several drafts). A few slight variations: for example, in the extreme right-hand figure.

68. BABYLONE D'ALLEMAGNE, coloured poster, 1,210 × 840 mm ($47^{5}/_{8} \times 33^{1}/_{6}$ in.) (L.D. 351), second state of two. The first state is before the lettering, which was certainly not done by Lautrec.

69. 9, PLACE PIGALLE, P. Sescau photographer, coloured poster, 600 × 800 mm ($23^{5}/_{8} \times 31^{1}/_{2}$ in.) (L.D. 353). Madame Bodelsen has pointed out that there exists a working proof of this poster in Copenhagen and in Albi, in which the woman is wearing a yellow mask.

70. QUI, L'ARTISAN MODERNE, coloured poster for Marty, 900 × 640 mm ($35^{7}/_{16} \times 25^{3}/_{16}$ in.) (L.D. 350). This state, which has not been described, comes between the second and the third states mentioned by Delteil, with the word *qui* and the drawing of draperies which were afterwards erased. Bibliothèque d'Art de l'Université de Paris.

71. BRUANT AT LE MIRLITON, coloured poster, 775 × 590 mm ($30^{1}/_{2} \times 23^{1}/_{4}$ in.) (L.D. 349), first state. Mme Bodelson has described several states.

72. LA LOGE AU MASCARON DORÉ (THE THEATRE-BOX WITH THE GILDED MASK), coloured lithograph, 307 × 241 mm ($12^{1}/_{16} \times 9^{1}/_{2}$ in.) (L.D. 16), first state.

73. AUX AMBASSADEURS, coloured lithograph for *L'Estampe Originale*, 302 × 246 mm ($11^{7}/_{8} \times 9^{13}/_{16}$ in.) (L.D. 68); 100 copies printed. Copy from one of the printings in olive green, belonged to M. Paul Prouté.

74. DANSE EXCENTRIQUE, lithograph for the catalogue of a poster exhibition at *La Dépêche de Toulouse* in May 1894, 178 × 129 mm ($7 \times 5^{1}/_{16}$ in.) (L.D. 67).

75. LE MODERNE JUGEMENT DE PARIS (THE MODERN JUDGMENT OF PARIS), drawing for *La Revue Blanche*, lithographed for a menu, 74 × 60 mm ($2^{13}/_{16} \times 2^{3}/_{8}$ in.) (L.D. 69). Very rare. Copy formerly in the Mutiaux collection.

76. MARCELLE LENDER IN 'MADAME SATAN', 344 × 250 mm ($13^{9}/_{16} \times 9^{13}/_{16}$ in.) (L.D. 58), second state of two. The play opened on 26 September 1893 at the Théâtre des Variétés. Lender reappears in 1895.

77. LA GOULUE AND VALENTIN, waltz. Music-title for Bosc, 298 × 230 mm ($11^{3}/_{4} \times 9^{1}/_{16}$ in.) (L.D. 71). 100 copies were published by Kleinmann before being reproduced for Bosc. There are printings in which Bosc's name is altered.

78. 'LA TIGE' AT THE MOULIN ROUGE, lithograph for Kleinmann, 280 × 250 mm ($11 \times 9^{13}/_{16}$ in.) (L.D. 70). Edition of 100 numbered copies. On the right, Maurice Guibert.

79. LA TERREUR DE GRENELLE (THE TERROR OF GRENELLE), 172 × 109 mm ($6^{3}/_{4} \times 4^{5}/_{16}$ in.) (L.D. 72). Edition of 100 copies, first state before lettering.
The subject is from *Gigolette*, a play by Tarbé and P. Decourcelle (November 1893), in which 'the fine world of street-walkers and apaches makes us spend an agreeable time' (*Le Triboulet*, 30 November).
The good proofs were numbered by machine.

80. LES VIEUX MESSIEURS (THE OLD GENTLEMEN), title of a monologue written by Maurice Donnay and created by Yvette Guilbert, 240 × 145 mm ($9^{7}/_{16} \times 5^{11}/_{16}$ in.) (L.D. 75), second state (with lettering) of three. The third state shows only the woman.

81. EROS VANNÉ (CUPID EXHAUSTED), title of a monologue by Maurice Donnay, created by Yvette Guilbert, lithograph, 275 × 200 mm ($10^{13}/_{16} \times 7^{7}/_{8}$ in.) (L.D. 74). One of the very rare copies of the first state (noted by Delteil) of four; the fourth shows Eros alone. According to M. Paul Prouté, the first state is the second, and vice versa, and 100 proofs of the first state were printed.

82. ADOLPHE OU LE JEUNE HOMME TRISTE (ADOLPHE OR THE SAD YOUNG MAN), title of a monologue by Maurice Donnay, created by Yvette Guilbert, 255 × 170 mm ($10^{1}/_{16} \times 6^{11}/_{16}$ in.) (L.D. 73), second state of two.
One of Yvette Guilbert's greatest successes; she sang it for thirty years.

It should be linked with the following lithograph. Both evoke the portrait of Lautrec's cousin, Tapié de Céleyran, from the point of view of style and posture.

83. ZIMMERMAN ET SA MACHINE (ZIMMERMAN AND HIS BICYCLE), 228 × 125 mm (9 × $4^{15}/_{16}$ in.) (L.D. 145), second state of three.
This work cannot be dated 1895, as Delteil did, for that was the year of Zimmerman's retirement to the United States (April). It must be dated 1894, the year of his triumph at the Vélodrome. The third state appeared in June 1895 in *La Revue Franco-Américaine*.

84. MENU HÉBRARD, 270 × 320 mm ($10^{5}/_{8}$ × $12^{5}/_{8}$ in.) (L.D. 66).
Adrien Hébrard (1833–1914); according to A. Flamant, Hébrard would often smile at his own jokes, 'surprised to find such a great number of them collected.'

85–102. YVETTE GUILBERT, text by Gustave Geffroy, illustrated by Toulouse-Lautrec, for Marty, album, approximately 265 × 178 mm ($10^{7}/_{16}$ × 7 in.) (L.D. 79–95). Title-page and sixteen plates, edition of 100. (No. 85 is a proof of No. 88, made prior to the text.)

103. YVETTE GUILBERT, in *Colombine à Pierrot*, song-title, 219 × 116 mm ($8^{5}/_{8}$ × $4^{9}/_{16}$ in.) (L.D. 96).
The printing of the first state coloured by Lautrec. M. Paul Prouté mentions a third state with lettering erased, coloured with stencil.

104. MISS IDA HEATH, English dancer, 360 × 265 mm ($14^{3}/_{16}$ × $10^{7}/_{16}$ in.) (L.D. 165). Only one state published by Kleinmann, printing of 100 on Japanese vellum, 20 on Chinese paper, and 30 on vellum.
A drawing at Albi is dated 1895 by Joyant.

105. CISSY LOFTUS, 369 × 246 mm ($14^{1}/_{2}$ × $9^{11}/_{16}$ in.) (L.D. 116), printing of 10 on Japanese vellum, and 25 on Chinese paper. Marie-Cecilia McCarthy (1876–1931), a Glasgow singer, was then 18 years old, and played male parts. Delteil wrongly dated this work 1895; Sagot had a copy dedicated by Lautrec to the model and dated 1894. It was exhibited at Brussels in 1895.

1895

106. NIB OU LE PHOTOGRAPHE AMATEUR, (NIB, OR THE AMATEUR PHOTOGRAPHER), illustration for a tale by R. Coolus in the *Revue Blanche* supplement, approximately 260 × 230 mm ($10^{1}/_{4}$ × $9^{1}/_{16}$ in.) (L.D. 99).
See Natanson on this supplement in *Peints à Leur Tour*, p. 271.

107. FOOTIT ET LE CHIEN SAVANT (FOOTIT AND THE PERFORMING DOG), 205 × 288 mm ($8^{1}/_{16}$ × $11^{5}/_{16}$ in.) (L.D. 97). Copy from the former collection of Mutiaux.

108. FOOTIT AND CHOCOLAT, 237 × 246 mm ($9^{5}/_{16}$ × $9^{11}/_{16}$ in.) (L.D. 98). Copy of the first state, before reduction, from the former collection of Mutiaux.
'...Chocolat, a dull-witted Negro in clinging black silk trousers and a red dress-coat, was an excuse for rough jokes and blows.
'With his big bare calves, his tasselled breeches, his starched collars, his flaxen locks, his harsh make-up, the grimace of his blood-red lips, his pointed hat from under which clouds of flour would fly when he got slapped, his sequin-covered bodices, his mad duchess's voice, his mixture of baby, nurse, and great English lady (his hairdo was a cross between Sarah Bernhardt's and Queen Alexandra's), Footit brought an atmosphere of the devil's nursery to the ring, in which children recognized their own sly, malicious tricks' (*Portraits-Souvenirs* by Jean Cocteau).
There is a forgery of this lithograph with a monogram in the bottom left-hand corner.

109. PROGRAMME FOR 'LE CHARIOT DE TERRE CUITE', 490 × 280 mm ($19^{5}/_{16}$ × 11 in.) (L.D. 77), second state with lettering.
On top is Félix Fénéon.

110. COVER FOR 'LE CHARIOT DE TERRE CUITE', by V. Barrucand, 176 × 112 mm ($6^{15}/_{16}$ × $4^{7}/_{16}$ in.) (L.D. 78), second state with lettering.

111. COVER FOR 'L'ESTAMPE ORIGINALE', 580 × 820 mm ($22^{13}/_{16}$ × $32^{1}/_{4}$ in.) (L.D. 127).

112. ANNA HELD, 320 × 200 mm ($12^{5}/_{8}$ × $7^{7}/_{8}$ in.) (L.D. 100), second state with lettering.
Anna Held had a long career. In 1913 (*Comœdia Illustré*, 20 March), 'The Americans are mad about her,' and she came to Paris to lecture on the *chic* of New York. She had married Florenz Ziegfeld in America.

113. YAHNE IN HER BOX, 320 × 170 mm ($12^{5}/_{8}$ × $6^{11}/_{16}$ in.) (L.D. 111); 25 copies printed.

114. YAHNE ET MAYER EN COSTUME DE VÉLO (YAHNE AND MAYER IN BICYCLING DRESS), in *L'Age Difficile* by Jules Lemaître, 328 × 220 mm ($12^{15}/_{16}$ × $8^{11}/_{16}$ in.) (L.D. 113). 25 copies printed.

115. LA REVUE BLANCHE, coloured poster, 1,300 × 950 mm ($51^{3}/_{16}$ × $37^{3}/_{8}$ in.) (L.D. 355), second state with lettering.
Mme Thadée Natanson, wife of one of the founders.

116. MAY BELFORT, coloured poster, 788 × 600 mm (31 × $23^{5}/_{8}$ in.) (L.D. 354), second state, without mark. The mark on the first state is a cat. A third state gives the address of the Petit Casino. A working state has coloured lines across the dress.

117. YAHNE AND ANTOINE, in *L'Age Difficile*, 330 × 260 mm (13 × $10^{1}/_{4}$ in.) (L.D. 112); 25 copies printed.

118. MAY BELFORT EN CHEVEUX (MAY BELFORT WITH HER HAIR DOWN), lithograph published by Kleinmann, 300 × 210 mm $11^{13}/_{16}$ × $8^{1}/_{4}$ in.) (L.D. 118), printing of 20 copies.

119. MAY BELFORT, trial for the large plate, 435 × 317 mm ($17^{1}/_{8}$ × $12^{1}/_{2}$ in.) (L.D. 120), only a few copies printed.

120. MAY BELFORT, another trial, 487 × 223 mm ($19^{3}/_{16}$ × $8^{3}/_{4}$ in.) (L.D. 121), only a few copies printed.

121. MAY BELFORT SALUANT (MAY BELFORT BOWING), another trial, 380 × 260 mm ($14^{15}/_{16}$ × $10^{1}/_{4}$ in.) (L.D. 117), 60 copies printed.

122. MAY BELFORT, large plate, 530 × 418 mm ($20^{7}/_{8}$ × $16^{7}/_{16}$ in.) (L.D. 119). The first state (Delteil's first state), including the people in the foreground, was issued by Kleinmann. The second state (Delteil's second state) is without the people. L.D. 122 seems to be a trial state or proof, but not a different plate, as M. Charles Pérussaux considered.

123. INVITATION ALEXANDRE NATANSON, 275 × 155 mm ($10^{13}/_{16}$ × $6^{1}/_{8}$ in.) (L.D. 101), first state of two, before lettering.
On the subject of this invitation see T. Natanson's *Peints à Leur Tour*, p. 252–258, and the memoirs of F. Jourdain. Jules Huret, of *Figaro*, who had not been invited, made fun of the invitation which was composed in English, 'asking if they wouldn't be using Hebrew next'.

124. MAY BELFORT AT THE IRISH AND AMERICAN BAR, Rue Royale, 320 × 258 mm ($12^{5}/_{8}$ × $10^{3}/_{16}$ in.) (L.D. 123). 20 copies printed. *Burlington Magazine* of June 1961 reproduced a copy that had on it the words: 'Respects to Miss Belfort after tormenting her for an hour.'
At first, Sagot thought this was of the Nouveau Cirque bar.

125. IDA HEATH IN A BAR, 329 × 225 mm ($12^{15}/_{16}$ × $8^{7}/_{8}$ in.) (L.D. 59).
Delteil dated this lithograph 1894; yet it must be put side by side with our 124, being similar in style as well as in size. It was published by Kleinmann, and 10 copies of it were printed.

126. BRASSEUR'S ENTRANCE IN 'CHILPÉRIC', 372 × 259 mm ($14^{5}/_{8}$ × $10^{3}/_{16}$ in.) (L.D. 110), second state with monogram, 25 copies printed for Kleinmann.
Chilpéric, an operetta by Hervé, was revived at the Théâtre des Variétés on 1 February 1895. Lautrec came to admire Marcelle Lender in it more than he did Brasseur.

127. LENDER DE DOS (LENDER SEEN FROM THE BACK), dancing the boléro in *Chilpéric*, 370 × 260 mm ($14^{9}/_{16}$ × $10^{1}/_{4}$ in.) (L.D. 106), edition of 20 copies by Kleinmann.

128. LENDER DANSANT LE BOLÉRO, DE FACE (LENDER DANCING THE BOLÉRO SEEN FROM THE FRONT), 367 × 260 mm ($14^7/_{16}$ × $10^1/_4$ in.) (L.D. 104), edition of 50 copies by Kleinmann.

129. LENDER DE FACE (LENDER SEEN FROM THE FRONT), 372 × 250 mm ($14^5/_8$ × $9^{13}/_{16}$ in.) (L.D. 105), edition of 25 copies by Kleinmann.

130. LENDER SALUANT (LENDER BOWING), 320 × 260 mm ($12^5/_8$ × $10^1/_4$ in.) (L.D. 107); 50 copies printed.

131. LENDER EN BUSTE SALUANT (LENDER BOWING, HALF-LENGTH) (L.D. 102), first state in black and white (print coloured by Lautrec). The plate of the first state is very large, 380 × 300 mm ($14^{15}/_{16}$ × $11^{13}/_{16}$ in.), very rare. In the second state, the plate is reduced, 325 × 235 mm ($12^{13}/_{16}$ × $9^1/_4$ in.), with a line framing the picture; 100 copies printed. Third state in colour, in the German magazine *Pan*, with the words *Original Lithographie in acht Farben von H. de Toulouse-Lautrec.*

132. LENDER ASSISE (LENDER SEATED), 350 × 235 mm ($13^3/_4$ × $9^1/_4$ in.) (L.D. 163); edition of 20 copies for Kleinmann.

133. LENDER AND LAVALLIÈRE in a parody of *Fils de l'Arétin*(?), 450 × 350 mm ($17^3/_4$ × $13^3/_4$ in.) (L.D. 164), second state, rare, Lavallière erased. Of the first state, with Lavallière, 20 copies were printed.
In December 1895, Mounet-Sully scored a great success as Arétin in *Le Fils de l'Arétin*, by Henri de Bornier, at the Comédie-Française. J. P. Laurens did a famous portrait of him. I believe that one should see here two distinct experimental sketches, rather than a parody of the play: first the portrait of Lender with a parasol, which did not satisfy Lautrec and which he erased, and a portrait of Lavallière playing Hamlet.

134. LENDER DEBOUT (LENDER STANDING), 350 × 240 mm ($13^3/_4$ × $9^7/_{16}$ in.) (L.D. 103). Copy from the printing of 15 in black for Kleinmann. Delteil mentions an additional printing of 12 in colour. There are some copies in black and white.

135. LENDER AND LAVALLIÈRE IN REVUE AT THE THÉÂTRE DES VARIÉTÉS, 303 × 245 mm ($11^{15}/_{16}$ × $9^5/_8$ in.) (L.D. 109), 25 copies printed.

136. AU PALAIS DE GLACE (AT THE ICE-PALACE), 255 × 245 mm ($10^1/_{16}$ × $9^5/_8$ in.) (L.D. 190), a few copies printed, experiment for a programme? Bibliothèque d'Art de l'Université de Paris.
Fin de Siècle (19 November 1896) announced that Jane Avril had recently started skating at the Palais de Glace: 'Her temperament, however, has remained just as explosive.' See a two-page spread on the Palais de Glace done by Willette in January 1896 for the *Courrier Français*.

137. LA BOUILLABAISSE, MENU SESCAU, 233 × 170 mm ($9^3/_{16}$ × $6^{11}/_{16}$ in.) (L.D. 144).
Supposedly a menu in honour of the photographer Sescau, a friend of Lautrec. Could it not be instead the dinner given for *Les Pieds Nickelés*, which had opened the previous night? Note the jokes strewn on the menu. Sescau played the banjo; he was photographed as a musician in the Molier circus. (Cf. No. 69.)

138. LENDER ET AUGUEZ DANS 'LA CHANSON DE FORTUNIO' (LENDER AND AUGUEZ IN 'FORTUNIO'S SONG'), 370 × 240 mm ($14^9/_{16}$ × $9^7/_{16}$ in.) (L.D. 108); 20 copies printed for Kleinmann.
The two women are acting in an 'opéra-comique' by Crémieux and Halévy, with music by Offenbach, at the Théâtre des Variétés. Fortunio, who has become a notary, is sixty years old. His young clerk, Valentin, sings to his wife, Laurette, the old song which was found in one of the files at the office. Catulle Mendès spoke about it in his column; 'Was Mlle Lender beautiful? You can be certain that she was! So much so that all were convinced she sang in tune. Mme Auguez whispered her song to perfection.'

139. LUCE MYRÈS DE FACE (LUCE MYRÈS SEEN FROM THE FRONT), 347 × 210 mm ($13^{11}/_{16}$ × $8^1/_4$ in.) (L.D. 125); 20 copies printed for Kleinmann.
In a revival of *La Périchole* at the Théâtre des Variétés.

140. LUCE MYRÈS DE PROFIL (PROFILE OF LUCE MYRÈS), 228 × 220 mm (9 × $8^{11}/_{16}$ in.) (L.D. 124); 20 copies printed for Kleinmann.
Same role. Maître Loncle owned a copy signed by Luce Myrès.

141. MLLE POIS VERT, 180 × 178 mm ($7^1/_{16}$ × 7 in.) (L.D. 126); 25 copies printed in green tones.
There is a drawing of the same person seen from the front at Albi.

142. LES PIEDS NICKELÉS, cover for the text of the play by Tristan Bernard, staged on 15 March 1895, published by Ollendorff, May 1895. 190 × 250 mm ($7^1/_2$ × $9^{13}/_{16}$ in.) (L.D. 128), first state, before lettering.

143. LE BÉZIGUE *(La Belle et la Bête)*, novella by Coolus, 310 × 260 mm ($12^3/_{16}$ × $10^1/_4$ in.) (L.D. 115), rare, unpublished print. Former collection of Mutiaux.
This print was reproduced in *Le Figaro Illustré* in September 1895. It was an illustration for a tale by Romain Coolus.

144. AU VÉLODROME (AT THE BICYCLE RACE-TRACK), 420 × 550 mm ($16^9/_{16}$ × $21^5/_8$ in.) (L.D. 146), not published, very rare.
Simpson the bicycle-designer and Mickaël the racer.
J. Bernard was sports director at the Vélodrome, and had given Lautrec access to it.
'Mickaël represents a unique type, for his performance is good only when he is forced on by his trainers, and he can do absolutely nothing as soon as he is left on his own. It's curious to watch, but of practically no interest as sport' (*L'Abbé Cane* in *Gil Blas*, 1 March 1896).
Simpson and his representative Bouglé later commissioned Lautrec to do a poster for them (cf. No. 184).

145. AU VÉLODROME, 310 × 460 mm ($12^3/_{16}$ × $18^1/_8$ in.) (L.D. 147), unpublished, very rare.

146. LA GOULUE DEVANT LE TRIBUNAL (LA GOULUE AT THE TRIAL), 253 × 230 mm ($9^{15}/_{16}$ × $9^1/_{16}$ in.) (L.D. 148).
La Goulue, looking strangely rejuvenated, does not appear here as the accused, but as a witness for the prosecution, which amused Lautrec. She was no longer dancing, but showed performing animals. The trial took place at the instigation of Senator Béranger's *Ligue Morale*, charging a certain number of young painters and their models with indecent conduct at the *Bal Fin de Siècle* at the Elysée-Montmartre. The story caused something of a stir; a street fight in the Latin Quarter resulted in the death of several persons.
During the trial, La Goulue explained that she had 'lightened' her dress so as not to be in contrast with this milieu which was more easy-going than her own; she was becoming more respectable, and had long discussions with a priest in Montmartre.

147. LA CHÂTELAINE, 567 × 452 mm ($22^5/_{16}$ × $17^{13}/_{16}$ in.) (L.D. 357), first state before lettering.
Poster for a novel which came out in *La Dépêche de Toulouse*.

148. UN MONSIEUR ET UNE DAME (A LADY AND A GENTLEMAN), programme for *L'Argent*, by Fabre, 350 × 270 mm ($13^3/_4$ × $10^5/_8$ in.) (L.D. 15), first state, before lettering. The second state is in colour and smaller (320 × 238) ($12^5/_8$ × $9^3/_8$ in.).
Delteil is wrong to date this programme 1893, for it was actually done for the opening of the play, on 5 May 1895. Arquillière and Mme Henriot acted in it. Fabre's subject was the question of an inheritance which the children eagerly await and want to take away from the mother, Mme Reynard (seen here, from the back, with her husband, who makes chocolate 'out of just about anything'). Looked upon as the 'masterpiece of cynical comedy', it was a success; *La Revue Blanche* (1895, I, p. 479), *La Vie Parisienne* (11 May) and *Le Courrier Français* (12 May) reviewed it, mainly agreeing that it was too sombre, and claiming that there weren't that many monsters in the world. Jules Lemaître, who agreed with this, compared it to Becque's famous play, saying it was 'all *Crows*, no doves'. He added that the play 'dated' a little. But Becque was the one who had recommended it two years previously to Antoine, who had had to postpone staging it until his return to Paris in the spring of 1895.

149. MAY MILTON, coloured poster, 785 × 597 mm ($30^{15}/_{16}$ × $23^1/_2$ in.) (L.D. 356), second state without mark in black; 100 copies printed.
The poster was done for a tour of the United States, but it was not used in the streets of Paris. *Le Rire* was given exclusive permission to reproduce it on 3 August 1895.
According to M. Prouté, one comes across prints in black only.

150. NAPOLÉON, projected coloured poster, 590 × 452 mm ($23^1/_4$ × $17^{13}/_{16}$ in.) (L.D. 358), 100 copies printed.
A competition had been organized for the illustration of a book on Napoleon, by W. Milligan Sloane, which was to come out in New York. Lautrec won nothing (the results were announced in September in *Le Figaro*), and he had 100 copies of the poster printed for himself.

151. LE SECRET, song-title, 248 × 183 mm ($9^3/_4$ × $7^3/_{16}$ in.) (L.D. 135), first state before lettering, 50 copies printed.
Here begins a set of 14 song-titles by Dihau. Dihau refused a set produced by another artist, preferring Lautrec's work. Of the first state, before lettering, 50 were printed. There are three more states with lettering and different printers' ad-

dresses: the first has the printer Bigeard, with the music on the back; the second has the printer Crenel; the third the firm of Crenel *frères*; the fourth does not carry the name of a printer (one or two printings).

152. BERCEUSE, song-title dedicated to Mme Zola, 248 × 192 mm ($9^{3}/_{4} \times 7^{9}/_{16}$ in.) (L.D. 141), first state.

153. CE QUE DIT LA PLUIE (WHAT THE RAIN SAYS), song-title, 166 × 178 mm ($6^{9}/_{16} \times 7$ in.) (L.D.131), first state.

154. LES PAPILLONS (THE BUTTERFLIES), song-title, 210 × 190 mm ($8^{1}/_{4} \times 7^{1}/_{2}$ in.) (L.D. 133), first state.

155. L'HARENG SAUR (THE SALTED HERRING), song-title, 228 × 208 mm ($9 \times 8^{3}/_{16}$ in.) (L.D. 134), first state.

156. LES HIRONDELLES DE MER (THE SEA SWALLOWS), song-title, 212 × 193 mm ($8^{3}/_{8} \times 7^{5}/_{8}$ in.) (L.D. 138), second state.

157. OCEANO NOX, song-title, 259 × 209 mm ($10^{3}/_{16} \times 8^{1}/_{4}$ in.) (L.D. 137), first state.

158. ADIEU, title for a boat-song, 236 × 193 mm ($9^{5}/_{16} \times 7^{5}/_{8}$ in.) (L.D. 129), first state.

159. BALLADE DE NOËL (CHRISTMAS BALLAD), song-title, 242 × 189 mm ($9^{1}/_{2} \times 7^{7}/_{16}$ in.) (L.D. 130), second state.

160. VALSE DES LAPINS (THE RABBITS' WALTZ), song-title, 310 × 230 mm ($12^{3}/_{16} \times 9^{1}/_{16}$ in.) (L.D. 143). Three states: the first in black before the complete lettering, containing the words 'La Valse des Lapins'. The second state has lettering at the top and bottom 'paroles de Dirocher, musique de Dihau, chez Bosc...'
Reprint by Edouard-Joseph with a change of the printer's address.

161. ÉTOILES FILANTES (SHOOTING STARS), song-title, 262 × 206 mm ($10^{5}/_{16} \times 8^{1}/_{8}$ in.) (L.D. 136), second state.
Dedicated to Maurice Guibert, whose face can be recognized here.

162. LES VIEUX PAPILLONS (THE OLD BUTTERFLIES), title for a minuet, 238 × 198 mm ($9^{3}/_{8} \times 7^{13}/_{16}$ in.) (L.D. 142), second state.

163. LE FOU (THE MADMAN), song-title, 228 × 148 mm ($9 \times 5^{13}/_{16}$ in.) (L.D. 132), second state, with lettering.

164. FLORÉAL, title for a sung waltz, 326 × 195 mm ($12^{13}/_{16} \times 7^{11}/_{16}$ in.) (L.D. 139), first state before lettering.

165. ACHETEZ MES BELLES VIOLETTES (BUY MY PRETTY VIOLETS), song-title, 235 × 173 mm ($9^{1}/_{4} \times 6^{13}/_{16}$ in.) (L.D. 140), first state before lettering.

166. SARAH BERNHARDT IN 'CLÉOPATRE', according to Delteil, or perhaps Loie Fuller, 283 × 242 mm ($11^{1}/_{8} \times 9^{1}/_{2}$ in.) (L.D. 150). First print (not numbered) of a set called *Treize Lithographies*, without text or publisher's name.
The circumstances of the publication of this set are not well known. Yet Sagot does mention that it was published by Sands, who handed it over to the Société des Amateurs Indépendants, which had 30 copies of it printed. It was bought up by Pellet, who offered 300 copies of it on 19 May 1906. There may have been a printing for the Vingt (or else copies reserved for them in 1895).

167. SUBRA, of the Opéra, or Sarah Bernhardt, 278 × 244 mm ($10^{15}/_{16} \times 9^{5}/_{8}$ in.) (L.D. 151).

168. CASSIVE, or rather Jeanne Hading, 240 × 242 mm ($9^{7}/_{16} \times 9^{1}/_{2}$ in.) (L.D. 162).

169. COQUELIN AÎNÉ (THE ELDER COQUELIN), 294 × 240 mm ($11^{9}/_{16} \times 9^{7}/_{16}$ in.) (L. D. 153).
Then aged fifty-four, it was in this costume that he played Molière's marquesses, and Sganarelle in *Le Médecin Malgré Lui*.

170. ÉMILIENNE D'ALENÇON, 294 × 242 mm ($11^{9}/_{16} \times 9^{1}/_{2}$ in.) (L.D. 161). Eve Lavallière?

171. YVETTE GUILBERT, or Lender, 298 × 246 mm ($11^{3}/_{4} \times 9^{11}/_{16}$ in.) (L. D.157). Rare print. Bibliothèque d'Art de l'Université de Paris.

172. JEANNE HADING, 289 × 245 mm ($11^3/_8$ × $9^5/_8$ in.) (L.D. 158).

173. JEANNE HADING, wrongly thought to be Lender, 295 × 242 mm ($11^5/_8$ × $9^1/_2$ in.) (L.D. 156).

174. CLÉO DE MÉRODE, 295 × 241 mm ($11^5/_8$ × $9^1/_2$ in.) (L.D. 152).
Cléo de Mérode had returned from abroad and was dancing at the Opéra-Comique. Her beauty and taste, as well as her affairs, were notorious. Gerbault drew a cartoon, called 'Le Jour du Roi' (*La Vie Parisienne*, 9 January 1897), which showed the King of Belgium ringing at her door.
Her flat headbands had created a fashion: 'Mlle de Mérode ought to be given compensation,' *La Vie Parisienne* suggested on 9 May 1896, 'everyone is imitating her headbands'; and Yvette Guilbert asked Jean Lorrain to write a song for her about 'the little pseudo-Botticellis with their flat headbands, all with little bellies starving at the opening-nights of the Œuvre and the Grenier de Montmartre'.

175. POLAIRE EN FILLETTE(?) (POLAIRE DRESSED AS A LITTLE GIRL), 290 × 240 mm ($11^7/_{16}$ × $9^7/_{16}$ in.) (L.D. 160).
Known as Eve Lavallière, she was perhaps the model for *Claudine*. She herself described her beginnings (*Comœdia Illustré*, 1 June 1909). After teaching herself to sing, she made her début at La Cigale, when she was very young. Six months later she was famous. 'I knew that I was strange rather than pretty, and I felt more capable of expressing emotion and passion than comedy. So what was I doing in a music-hall?' (Cf. No. 58.)

176. POLIN, 290 × 239 mm ($11^7/_{16}$ × $9^7/_{16}$ in.) (L.D. 159).
Polin was then at the peak of his career. His soldiers' songs delighted the public. He would sing them with hardly any movement, making 'a few lumbering steps in front of the prompter's box, his arms glued to his sides, or his hands resting on his knees'.

177. LUCIEN GUITRY, 295 × 242 mm ($11^5/_8$ × $9^1/_2$ in.) (L.D. 155).

178. JEANNE GRANIER, 298 × 242 mm ($11^3/_4$ × $9^1/_2$ in.) (L.D. 154).

179. JEANNE GRANIER, RIGHT PROFILE, 298 × 230 mm ($11^3/_4$ × $9^1/_{16}$ in.) (L.D. 265). Very rare proof, formerly in the Mutiaux collection.

180. JEANNE GRANIER, LEFT PROFILE, 286 × 235 mm ($11^1/_4$ × $9^1/_4$ in.) (L.D. 264). Wrongly dated 1899 by Delteil. Unpublished work. Bibliothéque d'Art de l'Université de Paris.

181. JEANNE HADING, first plate, 295 × 228 mm ($11^5/_8$ × 9 in.) (L.D. 262). Unpublished work, formerly in the Mutiaux collection.
Hading had acted at the Palais-Royal, the Renaissance, and the Gymnase; she had gone on tour abroad, had been a performer at the Comédie-Française (1892–1894), and had gone to act in America in 1894. *La Vie Parisienne* (1 April 1893) gave the following verdict on her limitations as an actress: 'She is very beautiful, but she has one fault: she only acts, and never projects an impression of real life.'

182. JEANNE HADING, second plate, 290 × 241 mm ($11^7/_{16}$ × $9^1/_2$ in.) (L.D. 263). Unpublished work. Copy from the Bibliothèque d'Art de l'Université de Paris. For no reason, Delteil dates this work and the previous one 1898.

183. PROGRAMME DE L'OEUVRE, 210 × 340 mm ($8^1/_4$ × $13^3/_8$ in.) (L.D. 149), first state before lettering.
See Lugné-Poë's *Acrobaties* (p. 140) on the importance of this programme-manifesto.

1896

184. CYCLE MICKAEL, projected poster, probably rejected, 800 × 1,200 mm ($31^1/_2$ × $47^1/_4$ in.) (L.D. 359); 200 printed.

185. 'LA LÉPREUSE', first staging of Bataille's play, 490 × 305 mm ($19^5/_{16}$ × 12 in.) (L.D. 196), second state with lettering. Portrait of Berthe Bady.

186. OSCAR WILDE AND ROMAIN COOLUS, programme for Théatre de l'Œuvre, 10 February 1896, 300 × 490 mm ($11^{13}/_{16}$ × $19^5/_{16}$ in.) (L.D. 195), fourth state.

Four states: the first before lettering, the second with the words 'l'Œuvre', the third with the lettering on the right-hand side, the fourth with the programme.

187. LA CHAÎNE SIMPSON, coloured poster, 860 × 1,280 mm ($33^7/_8$ × $50^3/_8$ in.) (L.D. 360). Kunstgewerbe Museum, Zürich. Was exhibited at Exposition d'Affiches Artistiques at Rheims in 1896.

188. LA PASSAGÈRE, coloured lithograph, 608 × 407 mm ($23^{15}/_{16}$ × 16 in.) (L.D. 366), first state before lettering. This lithograph was later used a a poster for the Salon des Cent. It was exhibited in Brussels at the beginning of 1896. As we know, it shows a young woman that Lautrec admired on a boat which nearly carried him off with her to Dakar.

189. IRISH AND AMERICAN BAR, poster for the *Chap Book*, 407 × 610 mm (16 × 24 in.) (L.D. 362).

190. SOUPER À LONDRES, came out in the first installment of *Etudes de Femmes*, published by Lemercier, 310 × 365 mm ($12^3/_{16}$ × $14^3/_8$ in.) (L.D. 167). Only one state, without lettering, 100 signed copies, in the *Etudes de Femmes*, printed by Lemercier for *L'Estampe Originale*, 1896. Hermann-Paul and Willette also participated in this publication. We give it the title as indicated in the table of contents of *Etudes de Femmes*, but collectors have given it various other names: *Five o'clock*, *Le Lunch*, *En Cabinet Particulier*.
In memory of Lautrec's trip to London in 1895.

191. PROCÈS LEBAUDY (LEBAUDY TRIAL), Mlle Marsy giving evidence, 460 × 485 mm ($18^1/_8$ × $19^1/_8$ in.) (L.D. 194). Unpublished lithograph. Three states: in the first, three people on the right; in the second state, neither the people, nor the date, nor the monogram; the third state is reduced, and contains four characters in all.

192. PROCÈS ARTON (ARTON TRIAL), Arton speaking in his own defence (and not Dupas giving evidence), 355 × 470 mm (14 × $18^1/_2$ in.) (L.D. 191).
'Drawn from life' (*Le Rire*, 4 April).

193. PROCÈS ARTON, DÉPOSITION DE RIBOT (ARTON TRIAL, RIBOT GIVING EVIDENCE), 410 × 570 mm ($16^1/_8$ × $22^7/_{16}$ in.) (L.D. 192).
Drawing at Albi; on the back is a study of the Rothschild coachman.

194. PROCÈS ARTON, DÉPOSITION DE SOUDAIS (ARTON TRIAL, SOUDAIS GIVING EVIDENCE), 450 × 600 mm ($17^3/_4$ × $23^5/_8$ in.) (L.D. 193).
Drawing at Albi; on the back: Choppy, the English bicycle trainer.

195. AU BAR PICTON, RUE SCRIBE, 330 × 233 mm (13 × $9^3/_{16}$ in.) (L.D. 173), 25 copies printed.
The Cosmopolitan American Bar, 4 rue Scribe, was managed by Achille Picton, who used to call Lautrec M. le Vicomte Marquis.

196. PORTRAIT OF DIHAU, dated 1896 by Delteil, 145 × 137 mm ($5^{11}/_{16}$ × $5^3/_8$ in.) (L.D. 176), unpublished work, probably intended to serve as frontispiece for Dihau's songs, more probably dates from 1895. Rare proof, from the former Mutiaux collection.

197. AFFICHE DE 'LA VACHE ENRAGÉE', coloured poster, 825 × 600 mm ($32^1/_2$ × $23^5/_8$ in.) (L.D. 364), first state with lettering.
The first issue of Willette's newspaper came out on 11 March, and continued until 1897. There is a different draft of this poster at Albi. It was reproduced in *La Plume* on 15 April 1896.

198. MLLE ÉGLANTINE'S TROUPE, coloured poster, for a tour of England, 615 × 800 mm ($24^1/_4$ × $31^1/_2$ in.) (L.D. 361), third state, with lettering (the two first states are before lettering; the first has a mark).
The poster was reproduced in *Le Courrier Français* of 16 February.

199. AU CONCERT, small coloured poster for the Ault & Wiborg ink company, 320 × 250 mm($12^5/_8$ × $9^{13}/_{16}$ in.) (L.D. 365). The first state before lettering, the second with the copyright, the third with text. The zinc plate has been preserved at the Art Institute of Chicago, which had a printing of 100 made in 1946.

200. FRONTISPIECE OF 'ELLES', coloured lithograph, 510 × 390 mm ($20\frac{1}{16} \times 15\frac{3}{8}$ in.) (L.D. 179). 100 copies of this set were printed. The title-page was also used as a poster.
There is a reproduction, in slightly reduced dimensions, of the series with border, done by Gründ before the war.

201. ELLES, LA CLOWNESSE ASSISE (THE SEATED CLOWNESS), coloured lithograph, 520 × 400 mm ($20\frac{1}{2} \times 15\frac{3}{4}$ in.) (L.D. 180). Several states exist, one annotated at the Bibliothèque Nationale.

202. ELLES, FEMME AU PLATEAU (WOMAN WITH TRAY), coloured lithograph (Mme Baron and Mlle Popo), 403 × 520 mm ($15\frac{7}{8} \times 20\frac{1}{2}$ in.) (L.D. 181).
Mme Juliette Baron, born at Chaumont, was the mother of Paulette, known as Popo, who was kept by Paul Guibert. Proofs in black and sepia.

203. ELLES, FEMME COUCHÉE (WOMAN IN BED), coloured lithograph, 400 × 518 mm ($15\frac{3}{4} \times 20\frac{3}{8}$ in.) (L.D. 182).

204. ELLES, FEMME AU TUB (WOMAN WITH TUB), coloured lithograph, 400 × 520 mm ($15\frac{3}{4} \times 20\frac{1}{2}$ in.) (L.D. 183). There are copies in black, in sepia, and in colours.

205. ELLES, FEMME QUI SE LAVE (WOMAN WASHING HERSELF), coloured lithograph, 520 × 400 mm ($20\frac{1}{2} \times 15\frac{3}{4}$ in.) (L.D. 184).
There are copies in sepia, in green, and on old-rose paper.

206. ELLES, FEMME À LA GLACE (WOMAN AT THE MIRROR), coloured lithograph, 520 × 400 mm ($20\frac{1}{2} \times 15\frac{3}{4}$ in.) (L.D. 185).

207. ELLES, FEMME QUI SE PEIGNE (WOMAN COMBING HER HAIR), coloured lithograph, 520 × 385 mm ($20\frac{1}{2} \times 15\frac{3}{16}$ in.) (L.D. 186).
Printed on four different papers.

208. ELLES, FEMME AU LIT (WOMAN IN BED), profile (same models as in No. 202), coloured lithograph, 400 × 520 mm ($15\frac{3}{4} \times 20\frac{1}{2}$ in.) (L.D. 187). Printed on old-rose and cream-coloured paper.

209. ELLES, FEMME EN CORSET, also known as *Conquête de Passage* (A Passing Fancy), coloured lithograph, 520 × 400 mm ($20\frac{1}{2} \times 15\frac{3}{4}$ in.) (L.D. 188).

210. ELLES, FEMME SUR LE DOS, LASSITUDE (WOMAN LYING ON HER BACK), coloured lithograph, 410 × 510 mm ($16\frac{1}{8} \times 20\frac{1}{16}$ in.) (L.D. 189).

211. LE SOMMEIL (SLEEP), coloured lithograph, 205 × 320 mm ($8\frac{1}{16} \times 12\frac{5}{8}$ in.) (L.D. 170), 12 copies printed.

212. DÉBAUCHE, 235 × 320 mm ($9\frac{1}{4} \times 12\frac{5}{8}$ in.) (L.D. 178).
A curious work. Perhaps Lautrec added the man, his friend Dethomas, at the request of a publisher. Cover for Arnould's catalogue of artistic posters, 7 Rue Racine.

213. DÉBAUCHE, variant, 237 × 320 mm ($9\frac{5}{16} \times 12\frac{5}{8}$ in.) (L.D. 177).
Another version of the previous work. Perhaps with two women. Rare copy, from the Mutiaux collection.

214. BLANCHE ET NOIRE (BLACK AND WHITE), 450 × 288 mm ($17\frac{3}{4} \times 11\frac{5}{16}$ in.) (L.D. 171); 12 copies printed.
In the luxury copies of *Lautrec par Lautrec* by Huisman and Mme Dortu (1964), an original lithograph is claimed. It actually is a photo-lithograph derived from this work.

215. MARY HAMILTON, 267 × 118 mm ($10\frac{1}{2} \times 4\frac{5}{8}$ in.) (L.D. 175); a few copies printed. Former collection of Mutiaux. Lautrec had already drawn her in 1893.
A reprinting of this work exists, published by Frapier in 1925.

216. ANNA HELD AND BALDY, 306 × 236 mm ($12\frac{1}{16} \times 9\frac{5}{16}$ in.) (L.D. 168); 20 copies printed for Kleinmann.
'The inimitable Anna' was born in Paris, and died in New York in 1918.

217. LA LOGE PENDANT QU'ON JOUE 'FAUST' (THE BOX DURING A PERFORMANCE OF 'FAUST'), or *A l'Opéra*, 352 × 252 mm ($13^7/_8$ × $9^{15}/_{16}$ in.). (L.D. 166).

218. SORTIE DE THÉÂTRE (LEAVING THE THEATRE), 310 × 265 mm ($12^3/_{16}$ × $10^7/_{16}$ in.) (L.D. 169), 25 copies printed.
The madame of a brothel in the Rue des Moulins returns from the theatre, to which Lautrec sometimes took her.

219. AU LIT (IN BED), unpublished lithograph. Unknown size. The only copy disappeared during the war.

220. 'L'AUBE', illustrated review, poster, 525 × 705 mm ($20^{11}/_{16}$ × $27^3/_4$ in.) (L.D. 363).
L'Aube, an art review, must have started in April or May, for on 16 April, the director asked Goncourt to write a few lines for the first issue.

221. MENU DU DINER DES TARNAIS, 190 × 200 mm ($7^1/_2$ × $7^7/_8$ in.) (L.D. 197), rare copy before lettering. Formerly in the Mutiaux collection.

222. MENU SYLVAIN, 215 × 198 mm ($8^1/_2$ × $7^{13}/_{16}$ in.) (L.D. 198); only a small number of copies printed.
Maurice Guibert said that the dinner was given on the eve of his younger brother's marriage. Monod claims that it was actually a reception for Etienne Giraud.

223. LE SUISSE, menu for Georges Lasserre's bachelor-party, 365 × 265 mm ($14^3/_8$ × $10^7/_{16}$ in.) (L.D. 199). First state without lettering. Formerly in the Mutiaux collection.

224. LE CROCODILE, menu for a dinner given on 23 December 1896, 320 × 240 mm ($12^5/_8$ × $9^7/_{16}$ in.) (L.D. 200), second state, with lettering.
Maurice Guibert is seen taking Tapié de Céleyran's mistress away from him.
In a third state, Lautrec erased everything except the portrait of himself sitting on a folding-stool, and used the plate as a visiting-card.

225. MENU OF A DINNER AT MAY BELFORT'S, 18 Rue Clapeyron, 164 × 73 mm ($6^7/_{16}$ × $2^7/_8$ in.) (L.D. 201). Copy from the Joyant collection, in the Pellet sale in Zürich, 1962.

226. A MERRY CHRISTMAS..., May Belfort's Christmas card, 190 × 150 mm ($7^1/_2$ × $5^{15}/_{16}$ in.) (L.D. 202); a few copies printed.
Sagot saw a copy with the signature of May Belfort on it, and the date 1896–1897. May Belfort fell ill, and had to leave France, where she was never seen again.

1897

227. INVITATION À UNE TASSE DE LAIT DANS L'ATELIER DE LAUTREC (INVITATION TO HAVE A CUP OF MILK AT LAUTREC'S STUDIO), 265 × 205 mm ($10^7/_{16}$ × $8^1/_{16}$ in.) (L.D. 326). Wrongly dated 1900 by Delteil.

228. COVER OF 'COURTES JOIES', by J. Sermet, 188 × 247 mm ($7^7/_{16}$ × $9^3/_4$ in.) (L.D. 216), first state, before lettering.
The stone belonged to M. Frapier, who had another printing made.

229. LA GRANDE LOGE, coloured lithograph, 510 × 400 mm ($20^1/_{16}$ × $15^3/_4$ in.) (L.D. 204); 12 copies printed for Pellet.
In the foreground, Mme Armande (Mme Brazier), next to her, perhaps Mlle Baron; behind, 'the Rothschilds' coachman'. Charles Pérussaux has pointed out (*Lettres Françaises*, 17 February 1955) that three states were printed. The lithograph is derived from a painting.

230. IDYLLE PRINCIÈRE, coloured lithograph, 374 × 281 mm ($14^3/_4$ × $11^1/_{16}$ in.) (L.D. 206). Only one state, 16 copies printed for Pellet.
Allusion to the scandal of the day, the affair between the princess of Chimay, 'the most heavily made-up of princesses', with the gipsy Rigo.

231. THE CLOWNESS AT THE MOULIN ROUGE, coloured lithograph, 410 × 320 mm ($16^{1}/_{8}$ × $12^{5}/_{8}$ in.) (L.D. 205); 20 copies printed for Pellet.
The model is the same as the clowness in *Elles*. That first print had sold well, and it is possible that Pellet asked Lautrec to do a variant of it the following year.
A painting of this subject is in the O. Reinhart collection (1895).

232. ELSA LA VIENNOISE, coloured lithograph, 570 × 380 mm ($22^{7}/_{16}$ × $14^{15}/_{16}$ in.) (L.D. 207); 12 or 17 copies printed (an experimental copy shown here).

233. LES ROIS MAGES, song-title for Dihau, 355 × 250 mm (14 × $9^{13}/_{16}$ in.) (L.D. 293), second state, with lettering.
The style of this work suggests that it was done in 1897, and that it should be linked to *Sinaï*, although Delteil dated it 1899.

234. PROJECT OF FRONTISPIECE FOR A NEW EDITION OF GOYA'S 'DESASTRES DE LA GUERRA', 281 × 388 mm ($11^{1}/_{16}$ × $15^{1}/_{4}$ in.) (L.D. 295). Very rare copy from the former collection of Mitiaux.

235. COVER FOR 'LA TRIBU D'ISIDORE', by Victor Joze, 180 × 148 mm ($7^{1}/_{16}$ × $5^{13}/_{16}$ in.) (L.D. 215), first state before lettering.
This book was registered in November. (The picture is reproduced in the album supplement of *La Critique*, 5 November 1897.)

236. COVER FOR 'LE FARDEAU DE LA LIBERTÉ', by Tristan Bernard, published by *La Revue Blanche*, 163 × 165 mm ($6^{7}/_{16}$ × $6^{1}/_{2}$ in.) (L.D. 214), first state before lettering.

237. PROJECT OF FRONTISPIECE FOR 'AU PIED DE SINAI', 261 × 415 mm ($10^{1}/_{4}$ × $16^{5}/_{16}$ in.) (L.D. 246), very rare copy from the former collection of Mutiaux.

238. SCHLOMÉ FUSS AT THE SYNAGOGUE, lithograph for the luxury edition of *Au Pied du Sinaï*, 175 × 144 mm ($6^{7}/_{8}$ × $5^{11}/_{16}$ in.) (L.D. 247). Rare copy, from the former collection of Mutiaux.

239. UN CIMITIÈRE EN GALICIE (A CEMETERY IN GALICIA), *ibid.*, 185 × 151 mm ($7^{5}/_{16}$ × 6 in.) (L.D. 248), rare copy, former collection of Mutiaux.

240–250. AU PIED DU SINAI (AT THE FOOT OF SINAI), cover and ten lithographs, approximately 172 × 140 mm ($6^{3}/_{4}$ × $5^{1}/_{2}$ in.) (L.D. 235–245).
Lautrec illustrated this book by Clemenceau for the publisher Floury; a letter shows that he was working on it during the summer. The book came out in 1898.
I have grouped the lithographs according to their style and not according to their order in the book. They therefore correspond to the following page-numbers: p. 8, 54, 76, 40, 82, 22, 68, 36, 48, 92.

251. CULS-DE-LAMPE (ornaments for blank pages), for above work and not for the *Histoires Naturelles* (L.D. 320).

252. A LA SOURIS, CHEZ PALMYRE, 359 × 252 mm ($14^{1}/_{8}$ × $9^{15}/_{16}$ in.) (L.D. 210), first state, very rare, a little larger than the second, of which 25 copies were printed.
At the museum of Albi there is a drawing of Palmyre and of her dog.

253. MENU AU BULL DE PALMYRE, approximately 250 × 220 mm ($9^{13}/_{16}$ × $8^{11}/_{16}$ in.) (L.D. 211); a few copies printed. Former collection of Mutiaux (copy from Stern).

254. LE MARCHAND DE MARRONS (THE CHESTNUT VENDOR), 258 × 175 mm ($10^{3}/_{16}$ × $6^{7}/_{8}$ in.) (L.D. 335).
'Published in April 1901 by Edmond Sagot, 25 copies.' This information, supplied by Delteil, must be re-examined; April 1901 was the date of Lautrec's return to Paris, and not that of the drawing on this stone which dates from 1897, as Palmyre's bulldog appears in the foreground.
Delteil's mistake derives from a note Sagot made in his records that he had bought 17 copies in May 1901 and 4 in September. This shows he was concerned with the plate at that time, but not that he published it then.

255. AU BOIS, 332 × 246 mm ($13^{1}/_{16}$ × $9^{11}/_{16}$ in.) (L.D. 296).
Delteil dates this work 1899.

256. LE CHEVAL ET LE CHIEN À LA PIPE (THE HORSE AND THE DOG WITH THE PIPE), 130 × 190 mm ($5^{1}/_{8}$ × $7^{1}/_{2}$ in.) (L.D. 289), one of the few copies. Bibliothèque d'Art de l'Université de Paris.

257. LA PETITE LOGE, coloured poster, 250 × 337 mm ($9^{13}/_{16}$ × $13^{1}/_{4}$ in.) (L.D. 209), second state with the woman's hairdo touched up with 'crachis'.

258. LA DANSE AU MOULIN ROUGE, LES DEUX AMIES (THE TWO FRIENDS), large colour print, 460 × 350 mm ($18^{1}/_{8}$ × $13^{3}/_{4}$ in.) (L.D. 208); 20 copies pulled for Pellet.
Done after a painting dating from 1892 (Prague Museum).

259. CHEVAL ET CHIEN COLLEY (HORSE AND COLLIE DOG), 330 × 230 mm (13 × $9^{1}/_{16}$ in.) (L.D. 283). One of the rare copies of the second state (in the first state, the horse is black).

260. ATTELAGE EN TANDEM (DOUBLE HARNESS), 263 × 415 mm ($10^{3}/_{8}$ × $16^{5}/_{16}$ in.) (L.D. 218), one of the rare copies.

261. LE CHIEN ET LE LAPIN (THE DOG AND THE RABBIT), wrongly called *Le Cochon* by Delteil, approximately 300 × 210 mm ($11^{13}/_{16}$ × $8^{1}/_{4}$ in.) (L.D. 323).
This work shows the collie that appears in the preceding plates. The theme of *Histoires Naturelles*, by Jules Renard, begins to emerge in these works. Lautrec had suggested to Renard his illustrating the *Histoires* in 1895.

262. PROJECT OF COVER FOR 'HISTOIRES NATURELLES', 295 × 215 mm ($11^{5}/_{8}$ × $8^{1}/_{2}$ in.) (L.D. 321), rare copy with indication of the measurements for the intended book.

263. DÉCLARATION, first plate, 298 × 225 mm ($11^{3}/_{4}$ × $8^{7}/_{8}$ in.) (L.D. 327). Dated 1900 by Delteil. Very rare copy from the former Mutiaux collection.

264. 'ROSMERSHOLM' AND 'LE GAGE', programme for the Théâtre de l'Œuvre, 1897–1898 season, autumn 1897, 294 × 255 mm ($11^{9}/_{16}$ × $10^{1}/_{16}$ in.) (L.D. 212), this copy between Delteil's second and third states (which are before lettering). The bearded man is Frantz Jourdain, author of *Le Gage*.

265. VIEUX ET FILLETTE (OLD MAN AND LITTLE GIRL), a variation on Frantz Jourdain's beard, 240 × 135 mm ($9^{7}/_{16}$ × $5^{5}/_{16}$ in.) (L.D. 229), rare copy, from the former Mutiaux collection.

266. L'ÉPOUVANTAIL (THE SCARECROW), done on the same day as the preceding plate, according to Delteil, 282 × 175 mm ($11^{1}/_{8}$ × $6^{7}/_{8}$ in.) (L.D. 228), rare copy from the former collection of Mutiaux.

267. L'ÉPERVIER (THE SPARROW-HAWK), thought of for the *Histoires Naturelles*, about 300 × 210 mm ($11^{13}/_{16}$ × $8^{1}/_{4}$ in.) (L.D. 322), second state with monogram, very rare.

268. THÉÂTRE ANTOINE, programme of the 'Gémier benefit', 295 × 210 mm ($11^{5}/_{8}$ × $8^{1}/_{4}$ in.) (L.D. 221), first state, before lettering.

269. LE PREMIER VENDEUR DE JOURDAN ET BROWN (HEAD SALESMAN AT JOURDAN ET BROWN), 150 × 110 mm ($5^{15}/_{16}$ × $4^{5}/_{16}$ in.) (L.D. 223). Copy in olive green at the Mutiaux sale, May 1931, No. 159.
Jourdan et Brown was a well-known clothing store at the time. Francis Jourdain talks about it in his memoirs. Delteil thought that this might be a project for an illustration.

270. À LA MAISON D'OR, 120 × 160 mm ($4^{3}/_{4}$ × $6^{5}/_{16}$ in.) (L.D. 222). A copy printed in olive green, Mutiaux sale, May 1931, No. 158.

271. LE COMPLIMENT DU JOUR DE L'AN (NEW YEAR'S GREETING), 250 × 222 mm ($9^{13}/_{16}$ × $8^{3}/_{4}$ in.) (L.D. 217).

272. HOMMAGE À MOLIÈRE AU THÉÂTRE ANTOINE, 227 × 190 mm ($8^{15}/_{16}$ × $7^{1}/_{2}$ in.) (L.D. 220), first state before lettering.
A third state with the words 'Hors les lois' was used as the cover of a brochure which came out at Stock's in 1898.

273. COVER FOR 'L'EXEMPLE DE NINON DE LENCLOS', by Jean de Tinan, 190 × 278 mm ($7^{1}/_{2}$ × $10^{15}/_{16}$ in.) (L.D. 230), first state before lettering.

1898

274. MON PREMIER ZINC, BONJOUR MONSIEUR ROBIN (MY FIRST ZINC ENGRAVING, GOOD DAY, MR. ROBIN), dry-point etching, first of the series, 262 × 117 mm ($10^{5}/_{16}$ × $4^{5}/_{8}$ in.) (L.D. 1).
Robin was a neighbour who lived on Lautrec's floor. He had become a friend and a sound adviser to Lautrec.

275. FRANCIS JOURDAIN, dry-point etching, 170 × 102 mm ($6^{11}/_{16}$ × 4 in.) (L.D. 4); 15 copies printed, along with the following dry-point etchings (276–282) in album form, for Manzi et Joyant, 1911.
Francis Jourdain, son of Frantz, has often spoken of Lautrec in a perceptive and sensitive fashion.

276. UNIDENTIFIED PORTRAIT (ARTHUR MEYER?), dry-point etching, 170 × 105 mm ($6^{11}/_{16}$ × $4^{1}/_{8}$ in.) (L.D. 8).

277. W. H. B. SANDS, PUBLISHER OF PRINTS, dry-point etching, 259 × 118 mm ($10^{3}/_{16}$ × $4^{5}/_{8}$ in.) (L.D. 5).
Sands commissioned Lautrec to do an album on Yvette Guilbert in 1898. He was the publisher of *Treize Lithographies*, in 1895.

278. LE LUTTEUR VILLE? ET DIVERS CROQUIS (THE WRESTLER VILLE? AND SEVERAL SKETCHES), dry-point etching, 157 × 120 mm ($6^{3}/_{16}$ × $4^{3}/_{4}$ in.) (L.D. 7).

279. THE EXPLORER VICOMTE DE BRETTES, dry-point etching, 170 × 87 mm ($6^{11}/_{16}$ × $3^{7}/_{16}$ in.) (L.D. 2).
Probably the explorer mentioned by Natanson. Lautrec took him about for a whole season, because 'he could tell everyone that he had fed on human flesh while he was in the Congo'.

280. LE PEINTRE-GRAVEUR CHARLES MAURIN (THE PAINTER-ENGRAVER, CHARLES MAURIN), dry-point etching, 169 × 98 mm ($6^{5}/_{8}$ × $3^{3}/_{4}$ in.) (L.D. 3); printed without burs.
See Natanson on the subject of this cynical draughtsman in *Peints à Leur Tour*, p. 166.

281. HENRI SOMM, dry-point etching, 170 × 103 mm ($6^{11}/_{16}$ × $4^{1}/_{16}$ in.) (L.D. 6).

282. TRISTAN BERNARD, dry-point etching, 168 × 100 mm ($6^{5}/_{8}$ × $3^{15}/_{16}$ in.) (L.D. 9); 25 copies printed for Tristan Bernard, then 445 more later to serve as an illustration in *Le Peintre-Graveur* of Delteil.

283. LAUTREC'S INVITATION TO AN EXHIBITION OF HIS PAINTINGS, 220 × 143 mm ($8^{11}/_{16}$ × $5^{5}/_{8}$ in.) (L.D. 232), very rare.

284. FEUILLE DE CROQUIS AVEC ADRESSE DE CALMÈSE ET SON CHIEN (SKETCH SHEET WITH ADDRESS OF CALMÈSE AND HIS DOG), 255 × 212 mm ($10^{1}/_{16}$ × $8^{3}/_{8}$ in.) (L.D. 336), rare copy from the former collection of Mutiaux.
Delteil dated this work 1901, without giving an explanation. We place it in context with the other plates on Calmèse.

285. CALMÈSE, SON CHEVAL ET SON CHIEN (CALMÈSE, HIS HORSE AND HIS DOG), 285 × 240 mm ($11^{1}/_{4}$ × $9^{7}/_{16}$ in.) (L.D. 291), 8 or 10 copies printed.

286. LE PETIT PONEY ET LE CHIEN DE CALMÈSE (CALMÈSE'S LITTLE PONY AND DOG), 248 × 300 mm ($9^{3}/_{4}$ × $11^{13}/_{16}$ in.) (L.D. 287); 15 copies printed.

287. LE CHEVAL ET LE COLLEY (THE HORSE AND THE COLLIE), 240 × 280 mm ($9^{7}/_{16}$ × 11 in.) (L.D. 288); one of the very rare copies.

288. L'AMAZONE ET LE TONNEAU (THE HORSEWOMAN AND THE CART), 233 × 290 mm ($9^{3}/_{16}$ × $11^{7}/_{16}$ in.) (L.D. 284); about 20 copies printed.

289. L'AMAZONE ET LE CHIEN (THE HORSEWOMAN AND THE DOG), 290 × 240 mm ($11^{7}/_{16}$ × $9^{7}/_{16}$ in.) (L.D. 285).

290. AU HANNETON, or *A la Brasserie*, 338 × 257 mm ($14^{1}/_{8}$ × $10^{1}/_{8}$ in.) (L.D. 272); 100 copies printed for Boussod, Manzi and Joyant.

291. AU LIT (IN BED), 310 × 253 mm ($12^{3}/_{16}$ × $9^{15}/_{16}$ in.) (L.D. 226); about 50 copies printed.

292. L'AMATEUR DE CHEVAUX (THE HORSE FANCIER), 232 × 238 mm ($9^{1}/_{8}$ × $9^{3}/_{8}$ in.) (L.D. 234); 20 copies printed.

293. AU CAFÉ, 297 × 137 mm ($11^{11}/_{16}$ × $5^{3}/_{8}$ in.) (L.D. 330), copy from the former collection of Mutiaux.
Delteil mistakenly dated this work 1900; it must be placed with the 1898 group. Delteil notes that the person represented here is the same as the one in the preceding work, J. Aclocque, son of a notary, and a great horse-fancier.

294. THE TILBURY, 245 × 242 mm ($9^{5}/_{8}$ × $9^{1}/_{2}$ in.) (L.D. 286). A very rare work, former collection of Mutiaux.

295. L'AUTOMOBILISTE (THE MOTORIST), 373 × 268 mm ($14^{11}/_{16}$ × $10^{9}/_{16}$ in.) (L.D. 203); approximately 15 copies printed.
Several of Lautrec's friends took an interest in the early days of the motor-car: Dr. Tapié, who can be seen here, and Paul Guibert, who was the first to do the run from Paris to Madrid.
Motoring was still so new that there were many who did not believe in it; yet by 1897 all the magazines gave it a column side by side with the bicycling column.

296. LE PETIT CHIEN (THE LITTLE DOG), *remarque*, 60 × 39 mm ($2^{3}/_{8}$ × $1^{1}/_{2}$ in.), only known copy. Print room of Brême museum.

297. MENU AU VIEUX, A LA FILLETTE NUE, AU CHIEN (MENU WITH AN OLD MAN, A NAKED LITTLE GIRL, A DOG), 205 × 185 mm ($8^{1}/_{16}$ × $7^{5}/_{16}$ in.) (L.D. 233); very rare copy, from the former collection of Mutiaux.

298. COVER FOR 'L'ÉTOILE ROUGE', by Paul Leclercq, 243 × 223 mm ($9^{9}/_{16}$ × $8^{3}/_{4}$ in) (L.D. 231), first state before lettering.

299. DÉCLARATION, second plate, 310 × 238 mm ($12^{3}/_{16}$ × $9^{3}/_{8}$ in.) (L.D. 328), copy from the Bibliothèque d'Art de l'Université de Paris. Delteil dates this work 1900.

300. LE VIEUX CHEVAL (THE OLD HORSE), 330 × 250 mm (13 × $9^{13}/_{16}$ in.) (L.D. 224); 50 copies printed.

301. PORTRAIT OF ADOLPHE ALBERT, 'the good engraver', 320 × 235 mm ($12^{5}/_{8}$ × $9^{1}/_{4}$ in.) (L.D. 273), second state with monogram. Registered at the Bibliothèque Nationale on 19 November 1898. 100 copies printed.

302. MARCELLE LENDER, 250 × 227 mm ($9^{13}/_{16}$ × $8^{15}/_{16}$ in.) (L.D. 261); 45 copies printed for Goupil.
An old theme, taken up again at the suggestion of Joyant.

303. DI TI FELLOW, 324 × 259 mm ($12^{3}/_{4}$ × $10^{3}/_{16}$ in.) (L.D. 271). Registered at the Bibliothèque Nationale in November 1898. 24 copies published by Boussod, Manzi and Joyant.

304. GUY AND MEALY IN 'PARIS QUI MARCHE', revue, 273 × 231 mm ($10^{3}/_{4}$ × $9^{1}/_{8}$ in.) (L.D. 270); 100 copies printed for Boussod, Manzi and Joyant.
This revue opened at the end of 1897.

305. EN SCÈNE (ON STAGE), 283 × 241 mm ($11^{1}/_{8}$ × $9^{1}/_{2}$ in.) (L.D. 213), copy from the former collection of Mutiaux.

306–316. YVETTE GUILBERT..., English set of eight plates, published by Bliss & Sands, London, in 1898, with cover, title-page and one unpublished plate, 300 × 240 mm ($11^{13}/_{16}$ × $9^{7}/_{16}$ in.) (L.D. 250–260). 350 copies printed on Holland paper. No. 308 is an unpublished experiment for Plate V: *Chanson Ancienne*, rare. Copy from the Bibliothèque d'Art de la Ville de Paris. Approximately 292 × 231 mm ($11^{1}/_{2}$ × $9^{1}/_{8}$ in.). Reprinted in 1930 by Brown & Phillips, London: 82 copies, of which 75 are in green, the first with plate outlines and inked in sepia. The stones are in the Albi Museum, which still uses one of the plates for reprints.
In her *Mémoires* (p. 126), and in *L'Art de Chanter une Chanson* (p. 95–96), Yvette Guilbert discusses the way she would interpret her songs. We see her here (L.D. 258) chiefly singing *La Soularde* (a masterpiece of interpretation, according to the *Courrier Français* on 7 October 1894) and *La Glu.* On her return from America, she had become an internationally known star. She had again taken up her 'dead white, at times terrifying mask'. Jules Renard described her in the following terms: 'her hair a shade of red that costs her, she says, 25 francs a month... a nose that would be convenient if one felt like kissing her on the mouth.'

317. PIQUE-NIQUE, 200 × 195 mm ($7^{7}/_{8}$ × $7^{11}/_{16}$ in.) (L.D. 174); only a small number printed. This work is in the style of Willette, who had asked Lautrec to do a poster, for his magazine, *La Vache Enragée* (Cf. No. 197). It is likely that this was an invitation to a picnic in the Paris suburbs; the Arc de Triomphe can be seen in the distance.

318. BICYCLISTES, project for a song-title(?), 248 × 223 mm ($9^3/_4$ × $8^3/_4$ in.) (L.D. 267), one of the few copies. Bibliothèque d'Art de l'Université de Paris (copy from Joyant).
One copy was inscribed by Lautrec to Sands (Cf. No. 277). This would seem to confirm my impression that this work was done between 1897 and 1898.

319. MME L..., OU CHEZ LA GANTIÈRE (MME L., OR AT THE GLOVE SHOP), 285 × 238 mm ($11^1/_4$ × $9^3/_8$ in.) (L.D. 225). Very rare. One copy was inscribed to Calmèse, according to Sagot.

320. DANS LA COULISSE (IN THE WINGS), 530 × 440 mm ($20^7/_8$ × $17^5/_{16}$ in.) (L.D. 268), a few copies printed at Bordeaux, according to Joyant.
Natanson says that Lautrec liked the Bordeaux Opéra because of its atmosphere, and not because of its performances. He felt the same way about the Comédie-Française.

321. BOUFFONNERIE À L'ANTIQUE (BUFFOONERY IN THE CLASSIC STYLE), 525 × 450 mm ($20^{11}/_{16}$ × $17^3/_4$ in.) (L.D. 114), approximately 30 copies printed.
According to Joyant, this work shows Mme Simon-Girard, Brasseur and Guy in *La Belle Hélène*. I thought it showed a revival of the play produced in November 1899, but M. Huisman dates the work as of Bordeaux about 1900. This would lead us to suppose that *La Belle Hélène* depicted here was the one with Mlle Cocyte. Delteil dated the work 1895.

322. LA CHARRETTE ANGLAISE (THE ENGLISH DOG-CART), or *La Partie de Campagne*, 1897. Colour lithograph for *L'Album des Peintres Graveurs*, 1897, by Vollard, 400 × 570 mm ($15^3/_4$ × $22^7/_{16}$ in.) (L.D. 219), experimental copy before the edition of 100.

1899–1900

323. JANE AVRIL, coloured poster, 560 × 360 mm ($22^1/_{16}$ × $14^3/_{16}$ in.) (L.D. 367), first state with the snake and before lettering; 25 copies printed (the second state has the name of Stern on it, and the snake has been removed).
This work is in the spirit of 1900, to be compared with the *Baiser au Serpent* by Dabault (Rheims, *L'Objet 1900*, p. 46 and 50).

324. LE PROMENOIR (THE FOYER), for *Germinal*, album published by *La Maison Moderne*, approximately 300 × 240 mm ($11^{13}/_{16}$ × $9^7/_{16}$ in.) (L.D. 290); 100 copies printed on Japanese vellum.

325. DANS LE MONDE (IN SOCIETY), 238 × 295 mm ($9^3/_8$ × $11^5/_8$ in.) (L.D. 329). A few, rare copies mentioned.

326. FANTAISIE, 272 × 239 mm ($10^{11}/_{16}$ × $9^7/_{16}$ in.) (L.D. 332). Former collection of Mutiaux.

327. CHIEN ET CHAT (DOG AND CAT), 138 × 293 mm ($5^7/_{16}$ × $11^9/_{16}$ in.) (L.D. 278). Rare copy, in the former collection of Mutiaux.

328. CHIEN ET PERROQUET (DOG AND PARROT), 305 × 262 mm (12 × $10^5/_{16}$ in.) (L.D. 277), second state, date '8 February 1899' erased. Bibliothèque d'Art de l'Université de Paris.
Since at least 4 January, Lautrec had been suffering from extremely severe psychic disturbances.

329. CONVERSATION, 276 × 190 mm ($10^7/_8$ × $7^1/_2$ in.) (L.D. 292), one of the rare copies, from the former collection of Mutiaux.
One letter mentions in passing a visit by Lautrec to La Souris (the bar shown in this work), on 14 February. He was interned in the nursing-home 'Madrid' at Neuilly from 17 March to 17 May.

330. AU CIRQUE, LE CLOWN (AT THE CIRCUS, THE CLOWN), monotype, 350 × 250 mm ($13^3/_4$ × $9^{13}/_{16}$ in.) (L.D. 337). Collection of Mme Dortu.
Like the two following works, this one was done by Lautrec at the Neuilly clinic to show that he was not mad.

331. AU CIRQUE, LA CLOWNESSE (AT THE CIRCUS, THE CLOWNESS), monotype, 50 × 33 mm (2 × $1^5/_{16}$ in.) (L.D. 338 *bis*).

332. JOYANT, monotype, 50 × 35 mm (2 × $1^3/_8$ in.) (L.D. 338). Collection of Mme Dortu.

333–355. ILLUSTRATIONS FOR 'HISTOIRES NATURELLES', by Jules Renard, approximately 230 × 180 mm ($9^{1}/_{16}$ × $7^{1}/_{16}$ in.) (L.D. 297 to 319). Done partly at the clinic, but begun earlier. The book, with 23 illustrations, was published in 1900 by Floury. 333 - cover; 334 - roosters; 335 - the guinea-fowl; 336 - the turkey; 337 - the peacock; 338 - the swan; 339 - ducks; 340 - the pigeons; 341 - the sparrow-hawk; 342 - the snail; 343 - the mouse; 344 - the spider; 345 - the toad; 346 - the dog; 347 - the rabbits; 348 - the ox; 349 - the donkey; 350 - the stag; 351 - the ram; 352 - the sheep; 353 - the bull; 354 - the pig; 355 - the horse.
In 1895, Lautrec had told Jules Renard of his wish to draw eight of the *Histoires Naturelles*, and he probably did several of them at that time. He then took up the subject again at the clinic, from March to May 1899, where Stern saw him drawing two plates from memory (the oxen of Céleyran, in the style of those done in 1881?). Neither Lautrec nor Renard was pleased with the other. Lautrec criticized him for dealing only with the well-known animals (Coquiot); Renard asked for illustrations to be redrawn; Lautrec replied that it was useless as, in any case, they did not have the same ideas about animals (Gauzi).

356. COUPLE AU CAFÉ-CONCERT, 162 × 315 mm ($6^{3}/_{8}$ × $12^{3}/_{8}$ in.) (L.D. 331); about ten copies printed.
Joyant dated this and the following pieces 1901. But Lautrec was no longer working then. It is better to place this group in 1899, after Lautrec left the clinic.

357. CLOWN ET CLOWNESSE APRÈS LE SPECTACLE (CLOWN AND CLOWNESS AFTER THE SHOW), 310 × 263 mm ($12^{3}/_{16}$ × $10^{3}/_{8}$ in.) (L.D. 324); 5 or 6 copies printed (3, according to Sagot) for Stern. Bibliothèque d'Art de l'Université de Paris.

358. AU STAR, LE HAVRE, 450 × 380 mm ($17^{3}/_{4}$ × $14^{15}/_{16}$ in.) (L.D. 275); 50 copies printed.

359. CHANTEUSE LÉGÈRE (CABARET SINGER), 310 × 255 mm ($12^{3}/_{16}$ × $10^{1}/_{16}$ in.) (L.D. 269); approximately 40 copies printed.

360. AU STAR, LA CHANSON DU MATELOT (AT THE STAR, THE SONG OF THE SAILOR) 340 × 260 mm ($13^{3}/_{8}$ × $10^{1}/_{4}$ in.) (L.D. 276), copy from the former collection of Mutiaux.

361. L'ENTRAÎNEUR (THE TRAINER), 240 × 450 mm ($9^{7}/_{16}$ × $17^{3}/_{4}$ in.) (L.D. 172). Approximately 40 copies printed.
Delteil put this work with those of 1896, without giving a date, which proves that he was uncertain.
Doucet bought his copy in 1911 at Sagot.

362. L'ENTRAÎNEUR ET SON JOCKEY (THE TRAINER AND HIS JOCKEY), 295 × 255 mm ($11^{5}/_{8}$ × $10^{1}/_{16}$ in.) (L.D. 281), rare copy from the former collection of Mutiaux.

363. LE JOCKEY SE RENDANT AU POTEAU (THE JOCKEY GOING TO THE POST), 388 × 282 mm ($15^{1}/_{4}$ × $11^{1}/_{8}$ in.) (L.D. 282), second state, with the trousers.
On one copy, Sagot read, in M. Lotz's handwriting, 'Last lithograph by Lautrec, unfinished, trial copy, unique. Only the green of the racecourse was left to fill in. Was taken to Stern's on 8 May 1902. Plate erased, etc.' (This copy from the Haviland sale, 2 June 1932, No. 104.)

364. LE PADDOCK, coloured lithograph, 360 × 320 mm ($14^{3}/_{16}$ × $12^{5}/_{8}$ in.) (L.D. 280), one of the copies printed in colour.

365. LE JOCKEY, or rather, as Guérin said, *Le Galop d'Essai*, coloured lithograph, 510 × 360 mm ($20^{1}/_{16}$ × $14^{3}/_{16}$ in.) (L.D. 279); 100, not 10, copies printed in black, and 100 in colour, for the publisher Pierrefort in the Rue Bonaparte.
Marcel Guérin bought his copy on 16 September 1901. Very deceptive reproduction by Edouard-Joseph.

366. LA GITANE (THE GYPSY), coloured poster, 1,600 × 650 mm (63 × $25^{9}/_{16}$ in.) (L.D. 368). Albi Museum.
The play was performed on 22 January 1900.

367. MISS DOLLY, DU STAR, or *La Petite Fille Anglaise*, July 1899, approximately 320 × 260 mm ($12^{5}/_{8}$ × $10^{1}/_{4}$ in.) (L.D. 274); only a few copies printed. Very close to a water-colour, in reverse, reproduced by Joyant, p. 203.

368. COVER FOR 'JOUETS DE PARIS', by Paul Leclercq, 210 × 98 mm ($8^{1}/_{4}$ × $3^{7}/_{8}$ in.) (L.D. 333), first state.

369. ZAMBOULA POLKA, music-title, published by Ondet, 223 × 210 mm ($8^{3}/_{4}$ × $8^{1}/_{4}$ in.) (L.D. 334), first state, before lettering, in black and numbered by machine, second state with the lettering in greenish black; third state, lettering obliterated by the numbering.

370. MME LE MARGOUIN, *Le Croquesi-Margouin*, 315 × 247 mm ($12^{3}/_{8}$ × $9^{3}/_{4}$ in.) (L.D. 325).
A young milliner with thick blonde hair, and a delicate face like a lively squirrel's. Lautrec called her *Croquesi-Margouin*, or just *le Margouin* (slang for 'mannequin'). With her, Lautrec was, according to Leclerq, 'like a child with another child. They understood each other.'
Also called *La Modiste*.